MORE PRAISE FOR *THE PRIEST OF PARAGUAY*

'Those who know little about South America and less about Paraguay will benefit greatly from this fascinating book.' *Bruce Kent*

'The complexities of Paraguayan politics are skilfully explored, as well as the complexities of the new president's personality, in all its contradictions. One would have to hunt far and wide to find a more useful analysis of contemporary Paraguay and its new leadership.' *Margaret E. Crahan, Kozmetsky Distinguished Professor, St. Edward's University*

'This book is a very readable account of the emergence of the person who has made Paraguay a country to be taken seriously again, and especially of the context – both political and ecclesiastical – that shaped him. An excellent introduction to Paraguay and its politics.' *Peadar Kirby, Professor of International Politics and Public Policy, University of Limerick*

'An excellent biography of Fernando Lugo ... Hugh O'Shaughnessy's expert knowledge of the deep divisions between traditional and progressive elements inside the Catholic Church also situates the "Lugo" phenomenon within the wider struggle for social justice in Latin America.' *Andrew Nickson, International Development Department, University of Birmingham*

ABOUT THE AUTHORS

Hugh O'Shaughnessy has been writing and broadcasting about Latin America for forty-seven years. In this time he has worked for the *Financial Times*, *The Economist*, *The New Statesman*, the *Observer* and the BBC, among others. He has won two British Press Awards and the Wilberforce Medallion from the city of Hull. He has also been recognized by the Columbia University Graduate School of Journalism in the United States. His books include *Grenada: Revolution, Invasion and Aftermath* and *Pinochet: The Politics of Torture*.

Edgar Venerando Ruiz Díaz is a Paraguayan journalist and news editor of the digital version of the Asunción daily *ABC Color*.

THE PRIEST OF PARAGUAY

Fernando Lugo and the making of a nation

Hugh O'Shaughnessy
and Edgar Venerando Ruiz Díaz

Zed Books

LONDON | NEW YORK

The Priest of Paraguay: Fernando Lugo and the making of a nation
was first published in 2009 by Zed Books Ltd, 7 Cynthia Street,
London N1 9JF, UK and Room 400, 175 Fifth Avenue, New York,
NY 10010, USA

www.zedbooks.co.uk

Set in Monotype Plantin and Gill Sans by Ewan Smith, London
Index: ed.emery@thefreeuniversity.net
Cover designed by Rogue Four Design
Printed and bound in the UK by the MPG Books Group

Distributed in the USA exclusively by Palgrave Macmillan, a division of
St Martin's Press, LLC, 175 Fifth Avenue, New York, NY 10010, USA

A catalogue record for this book is available from the British Library
Library of Congress Cataloging in Publication Data available

ISBN 978 1 84813 312 9 hb
ISBN 978 1 84813 313 6 pb
ISBN 978 1 84813 314 3 eb

CONTENTS

ILLUSTRATIONS

ACKNOWLEDGEMENTS

Thanks go to Ellen Hallsworth and Ken Barlow at Zed Books; Dionisio Borda; Ricardo Canese; Antonio Espinoza; Johannes Füllenbach, SVD; Margaret Hebblethwaite; Andrea Macháin; Francis McDonagh; Ricardo Medina; Andrew Nickson; Gerry O'Collins, SJ; Rubén Penayo and Michael Walsh.

No one attempting to write about Paraguayan politics can fail to have recourse to *ABC Color* as a daily record of the facts; no one trying to make sense of Stroessner can fail to read Bernardo Neri Farina's excellent book *El Último Supremo: La crónica de Alfredo Stroessner* (Editorial El Lector, Asunción, 2003).

ABBREVIATIONS AND ACRONYMS

ANR   Asociación Nacional Republicana, National Republican Association, the Colorado or Red party, founded with the Liberal Party in 1887

CDF   Congregation for the Doctrine of the Faith, successor to the Sacred Congregation of the Universal Inquisition, founded in 1542 and first renamed Sacred Congregation of the Holy Office in 1908. Given its current name in 1965

CDU   Christian Democratic Union, German political party formerly headed by Konrad Adenauer

CEB   Comunidade Eclesial de Base, Basic Church Community

CELAM   Consejo Episcopal Latinoamericano, Latin American Episcopal Council

EBI   Entidad Binacional Itaipú, Itaipú Binational Entity, joint Paraguay/Brazil company running Itaipú dam

EBY   Entidad Binacional Yacyretá, Yacyretá Binational Body, joint Paraguay/Argentine company running Yacyretá dam

ERP   Ejército Revolucionario del Pueblo, People's Revolutionary Army, Argentine guerrilla group founded in 1970, one of whose founders, Enrique Gorriarán, claimed responsibility for the assassination of Anastasio 'Tachito' Somoza in Asunción in 1980

FARC   Fuerzas Armadas Revolucionarias Colombianas, Colombian Revolutionary Armed Forces, founded by the Colombian Communist Party at its Tenth Congress in 1966

MSTM   movement of mainly Argentine priests formed in the 1960s at the time of Vatican II, later suppressed by the Argentine military, which seized power in 1966

NGO   non-governmental organization

OMI   Oblates of Mary Immaculate, male religious order founded in 1816

OP   Ordo Praedicatorum, the Order of Preachers or Dominicans

OPM   Organización Político Militar, Military Political Movement, guerrilla group set up in the mid-1970s inspired by the

Montoneros in Argentina and the Tupamaros in Uruguay, thought to have had some four hundred sympathizers. Armed action in Asunción in 1976 quickly suppressed by Stroessner forces

PLRA   Partido Liberal Radical Auténtico, Authentic Radical Liberal Party, formally founded in 1977 as a faction of the traditional Liberal Party

PPQ   Partido Patria Querida, Party of the Beloved Fatherland, political vehicle of Pedro Fadul, an independent left-winger who unsuccessfully contested the 2003 and 2008 presidential elections

SJ   Societas Jesu, the Society of Jesus male religious order, founded 1540 (Jesuits)

SOA   School of the Americas, US centre created in 1946 and initially sited in the Panama Canal Zone for training the Latin American military in strategy, tactics and torture. Graduates included senior officers who seized power from civilian governments. In 2001 moved to the US state of Georgia and renamed Western Hemisphere Institute for Security Co-operation

SVD   Societas Verbi Divini, Society of the Divine Word, founded in the Netherlands in 1875 by the German Arnold Janssens. Members known in Italy as '*Verbiti*' and in Spanish- and Portuguese-speaking countries as '*Verbistas*'

TSJE   Tribunal Superior de Justicia Electoral, Higher Tribunal for Electoral Justice, charged under 1992 constitution with responsibility for all electoral matters

UNACE   Unión Nacional de Colorados Éticos, National Union of Ethical Colorados, political vehicle for General Lino Oviedo, registered 1996

USAID   US Agency for International Development, founded by the US government in 1961

Vatican II   Second Vatican Council, 1962–65, proposed and inaugurated by the eighty-one-year-old Pope John XXIII in Rome

WACL   World Anti-Communist League, founded in Taiwan in 1966, inspired by Chiang Kai-shek. Provided funds for Stroessner

KEY FIGURES

Ageton, Admiral Arthur Ainslie (1900–71), US ambassador to Paraguay 1954–57

Antonini, Archbishop Orlando (born Villa Sant'Angelo, Italy, 1944), papal nuncio to Paraguay 2005–

Bogarín, Archbishop Sinforiano (1863–1949), archbishop of Asunción 1895–1949

Borda, Dionisio, minister of finance, Paraguay, 2008–

Chávez, Colonel Hugo (born Sabaneta, Venezuela, 1954), president of Venezuela 1999–

Cubas, Raúl (born Asunción, 1943), Colorado, president of Paraguay 15 August 1998–28 March 1999, political ally of General Lino Oviedo. Voted from office after assassination of Vice-President Argaña. Given political asylum in Brazil

Francia, José Gaspar Rodriguez de (1766–1840), Perpetual Dictator of Paraguay 1815–40

Las Casas, Bartolomé de, Spanish Dominican priest, born in the late fifteenth century, campaigner for rights of indigenous peoples

López, Carlos Antonio (1792–1865), president and modernizer of Paraguay 1844–65

López, Francisco Solano, president of Paraguay 1865–70, fought and lost war against Triple Alliance of Argentina, Brazil and Uruguay

Lula (Luis Inácio 'Lula' da Silva) (born Garanhuns, Pernambuco, Brazil, 1945), president of Brazil 2002–

Medina, Mario Melanio (born Fernando de la Mora, Paraguay, 1939), bishop of Benjamín Aceval 1980, co-adjutor bishop of San Juan Bautista de las Misiones 1997, bishop of San Juan Bautista de las Misiones 1999, ally of Lugo

Morales, Evo (born Isallavi, Bolivia, 1959), constitutional – and first indigenous – president of Bolivia 2006–

Oviedo, Lino (born Juan de Mena, Paraguay, 1947), Colorado, general and aspirant to presidency

Perón, General Juan Domingo (1895–1974), president of Argentina 1946–55, 1973–74

Pinochet, General Augusto (1915–2006), dictator of Chile 1973–90, detained on murder and torture charges in London then freed

Rodríguez, Andrés (1923–97), Colorado, commander First Army Corps 1981, president 1989–93

Rolón, Ismael (born 1914, Caazapá), bishop of Caacupé 1967–79, archbishop of Asunción 1970–89

Stiglitz, Joseph (born Gary, Indiana, 1943), chief economist at World Bank 1997–2000, Nobel Prize for Economics 2001, economics adviser to Lugo 2008–

Stroessner, General Alfredo (1912–2006), Colorado, dictator of Paraguay 1956–89

Taylor, Clyde (born Colombia, 1937), US ambassador to Paraguay 1985–88

Wasmosy, Juan Carlos (born Asunción, 1939), Colorado, president 1993–98

CHRONOLOGY

5000–4000 BC Establishment of Guaranís in South America

1492 First transatlantic voyage of Columbus

1536 Pedro de Mendoza founds the fort of Santa María de Buenos Aires with Spanish royal charter

1537 Asunción founded

1550 Goats introduced to Paraguay

1552 Cattle introduced to Paraguay. Bartolomé de las Casas publishes his *Brevísima relación de la destrucción de las Indias* (Briefest Account of the Destruction of the Indies)

1585 Jesuits found college in Asunción

1604 Jesuit General Acquaviva decrees the establishment of the Jesuit province of Paracuaria

1610 First reduction established in Paraguay at San Ignacio

1629–32 First attacks by *bandeirantes* from Portuguese territories in Brazil

1639 Pope Urban VIII confirms decision of Pope Paul III forbidding enslavement of Indians in America

1680 Up to 70,000 Guaranís living in Jesuit reductions and allowed by Spanish authorities to bear arms for defensive purposes

1723–35 Comunero revolt against Spanish viceroy

1767 Jesuits expelled from Spain and its colonies, 224 leaving Paraguay for Europe

1808–13 Joseph Bonaparte king of Spain

1810 Argentina declares its independence from Spain

1811 Paraguayans resist attacks from Argentines and appoint a provisional government

1816 José Gaspar Rodríguez de Francia declared 'Perpetual Dictator of the Republic' by congress of local notables in Asunción and cuts off almost all contact with outside world. Bans foreign travel and visitors from abroad

1840 Francia dies

1844 Carlos Antonio López declared President of the Republic for a ten-year period and starts modernization

1854–62 C. A. López's presidential terms extended

1858 Sixteen young Paraguayans sent to study in Europe

1861 First railway inaugurated

1862 C. A. López dies, Francisco Solano López inherits presidency

1864 F. S. López declares war on Triple Alliance of Argentina, Brazil and Uruguay. Paraguay invades Brazil

1865 Paraguay occupies Argentine city of Corrientes

1866 Paraguay loses strongpoint of Humaitá to Triple Alliance

1869 Asunción captured and sacked by Brazilians

1870 F. S. López and his two sons killed by Brazilian army. Occupied Paraguay starts paying heavy reparations

1875 Divine Word Missionaries founded at Steijl

1887 Foundation of the Liberal Party and of the Asociación Nacional Republicana (Colorados)

1894–1949 Sinforiano Bogarín archbishop of Asunción

1910–12 Rapid succession of six ephemeral governments

1912 Alfredo Stroessner born in Encarnación

1917 Epifanio Méndez Fleitas, Lugo's uncle, born at San Solano

1922 Civil war following coup attempt against President Eusebio Ayala, a Liberal

1928 Gustavo Gutiérrez, liberation theologian, born in Lima

1931–35 War with Bolivia

1940 General Higinio Morínigo takes power

1947 Brief civil war won by supporters of Morínigo

1948 Morínigo replaced

1949–52 Epifanio police chief of Asunción

1951 Lugo born at San Solano

1954 General Alfredo Stroessner assumes office, organizing fraudulent elections; confirms Epifanio as Central Bank president

1957 Puerto Stroessner (now Ciudad del Este) inaugurated

1959 Castro in power in Cuba

1962 Pope John XXIII inaugurates Second Vatican Council

1970 Lugo joins Divine Word Missionaries

1970–89 Ismael Rolón archbishop of Asunción

1973 Itaipú treaty signed by Paraguay and Brazil in Brasília. General Pinochet seizes power in Chile

1975 Operation Cóndor (Bolivia, Brazil, Chile, Paraguay, Uruguay) inaugurated

1976   Military coup in Argentina starts 'Dirty War'; Bishop Enrique Angelelli of La Rioja assassinated

1977   Lugo ordained priest of the Divine Word Missionaries

1978   Lugo sent to Ecuador

1979   Sandinistas overthrow Somoza dynasty in Nicaragua

1980   Archbishop Oscar Romero of San Salvador assassinated in San Salvador. Anastasio 'Tachito' Somoza assassinated in Asunción

1982   First electricity produced at Itaipú dam

1983–87 Lugo studying in Rome at Gregorianum

1989   Stroessner overthrown by General Andrés Rodríguez

1992   Lugo named head of Divine Word in Paraguay

1994   Lugo appointed bishop of San Pedro

1996   President Wasmosy arrests General Oviedo

1998   Oviedo freed by President Cubas

1999   Hugo Chávez becomes Venezuelan president. Paraguayan Vice-President Argaña assassinated, Oviedo flees

2000   Oviedo arrested in Brazil

2005   Lugo resigns from diocese

2006   Lugo heads mass demonstration against political fraud. Vatican admonishes Lugo for seeking presidency. Stroessner dies. Rafael Correa becomes Ecuadorean president. Evo Morales becomes Bolivian president

2007   Vatican suspends Lugo from episcopal functions

2008   Lugo wins election, receives gift from Pope Benedict XVI, is absolved of religious vows by Vatican and takes up presidency

2009   Lugo admits to fathering Guillermo Armindo, born 2007

TO GEORGIE

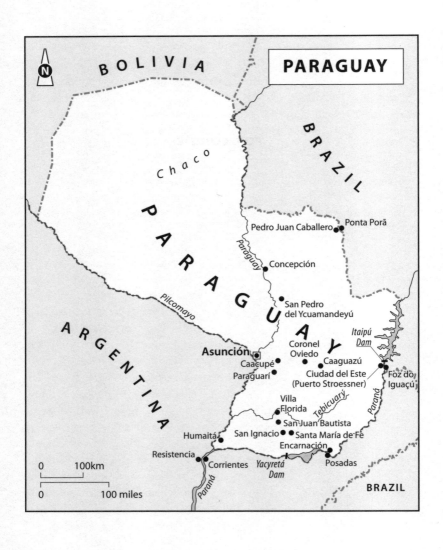

1 | THE BISHOP BECOMES PRESIDENT

On the pavement outside a modern former bank building in the centre of Asunción, the provisional headquarters of the Patriotic Alliance for Change, in early June 2008, armed troops stood on watch. A former bishop, Fernando Lugo, had just won the election for the presidency, pushing the governing Colorado party out of power for the first time in more than six decades. In front of the ground-floor reception desk milled a score of people seeking audience. Among them, a fragile group of octogenarians and nonagenarians, medals proudly worn on their best clothes, awaited their chance for a talk with the president. There are not many veterans left from the 1932–35 Chaco War with Bolivia, which left 36,000 Paraguayans dead and Paraguay narrowly victorious on the field of battle.

At the door of his office upstairs the sensation was one of political power. The British ambassador was ushered in. Then Dionisio Borda, Lugo's candidate for the economy ministry, appeared. Outside Lugo's inner office sat a beautiful secretary with long blonde hair: 'The president likes good-looking women,' said a friend. The buzz in the corridors, as the notables came and went, was the unmistakable one of state authority in the hands of one man. He was addressed as 'President' though there were some weeks to go before he was to don the sash of office.

The incoming leader of Paraguay, rimless glasses on his nose, informally dressed in a shirt without a tie under a brown jumper with patterns of llamas, and wearing mittens, received the visitor with a bright smile that lit up a bearded face. He showed all the aplomb and assurance of a man born to lead. He talked fast and with urgency. No small talk. No clerical pieties. Straight to the main questions and the careful but unhesitatingly trenchant answers from a man who gave the impression he knew what he wanted and had a fair idea of how to get it. The majority of his answers would not have shamed a left-wing social democrat in any country of the European Union in the twentieth century: a better sharing of the wealth between rich and poor; the need to educate the richer Paraguayans to realize that mass poverty was not their ally but a threat to their future; more respect for the constitution. At the end of his

1 Lugo (standing right) beside elder brother Pompeyo. Sitting, sister Mercedes (now First Lady) with baby, mother Maximina Méndez Fleitas de Lugo and father Guillermo Lugo Ramos.

five-year term, he said, a drive against political abuse would have helped Paraguay to become a 'serious' nation respected internationally.

All this was mixed with references to the sort of reforms needed in a country coming out of a long period of dictatorship – less corruption, a genuine agrarian reform, and one topic that would hardly be on the agenda of a politician in Europe: the state of the native peoples. 'I think', he said, 'that 1992, the five hundredth anniversary of the arrival of the Europeans, led to a rediscovery of the indigenes, their dignity and their very culture. There's a process of reappraisal going on.' This was clearly a man committed to doing something about the state of the indigenous peoples, whose treatment at the hands of the European conquerors and their descendants over 500 years had been a disgrace.

The man who was born in 1951 in a country village to a railway worker and his schoolmistress wife was preparing to take on the enormous task of modernizing one of the most backward countries in the world. Paraguay was not a poor country in the way that Honduras and Haiti were poor. Since the 1530s, when treasure-seekers and missionaries from Spain landed, it had been a colony where a small number of whites ruled over a mass of indigenous peoples, pastoral people, the majority speaking one or other forms of the Guaraní language. With the arrival of the Spaniards the missionaries among them made sure that the Christianity which they brought – and which was one of the reasons for the arrival of the Europeans – struck deep roots. Gold and silver were never discovered in Paraguay and it yielded none of the instant fortunes that other Spaniards found in Mexico and Peru. Yet there was plenty of land for its inhabitants. With plenty of water and a reasonable climate, that land produced plentiful food and the agricultural goods that the rest of the world later wanted to buy, notably meat and cereals.

Although Spain's colonial rule came to an end in the first years of the nineteenth century, Paraguay's trouble was that for the following two centuries many of the features of colonial society survived and it suffered from the scandalously bad distribution of income that was inherent in rule by the minority of whites and near-whites. Despite the efforts of a small group of missionaries to create a better society, which achieved fitful success, wealth was concentrated in very few hands, while the majority lived in deep poverty. The situation hardly improved when local leaders of European descent threw off rule from Spain at the beginning of the nineteenth century. Indeed, in many respects it worsened.

The prostration of large parts of Paraguayan society had not arisen because most Paraguayans were idle and lacking in initiative – they were not. Millions of them ended up emigrating to other countries where their industriousness was sought, though it was often badly rewarded. The difficulties of Paraguayans stemmed mainly from the fact that the rich continued to protect their privileges as they had over the centuries, in latter days refusing to pay taxes to provide the minimum standards of welfare which were taken for granted in other countries.

From 1947 until 2008 the same political party, the Asociación Nacional Republicana, or National Republican Association, universally known as the Colorados or Reds, had maintained the status quo and kept itself in power through a combination of trickery, corruption and terror.

Their most notorious leader, General Alfredo Stroessner, maintained himself as a dictator from 1954 to 1989. He had enjoyed the overt support of the dictatorships that flowered and died in neighbouring Latin American republics – Argentina, Bolivia, Brazil, Chile and Uruguay – and the backing of Western governments, which was no less effective for being largely hidden. Since the military coup that overthrew Stroessner in 1989, and despite the murderous rivalries among their leaders, the Colorados had maintained their power and the social system, which favoured a small minority. It took Lugo to start changing all that.

This is an account of how a talented and determined young man, who grew up in a pious Catholic family during the days of Stroessner, resolved to do what he could to better the grievous situation. After all, the state in which Paraguay found itself was in no small part the responsibility of his Church. The country took shape as a colony of a European power and was moulded by the ideas of Christianity brought over by Europeans. Fernando Lugo therefore resolved to help do away with the scorn to which centuries of colonialism and decades of mis-government had reduced it. He studied and worked hard, made his mark in the Church and the wider society, becoming associated with the founders of liberation theology, which was growing stronger in the atmosphere of openness that surrounded the convening of the Second Vatican Council by Pope John XXIII in 1962. He was named the bishop of a poor diocese, and in his middle years decided he could be most effective as a politician rather than as a cleric.

THE INAUGURATION

The accession to the Paraguayan presidency on 15 August 2008 of Lugo, once a bishop of the Catholic diocese, marked not just a further strengthening of the reform movement in Latin America to which others, such as Lula of Brazil, Chávez of Venezuela, Morales of Bolivia and Correa of Ecuador, had already contributed, and which was enjoying the benefits of favourable economic circumstances in the region. It also signified the happy re-emergence of the sort of reforms that had been championed for decades by liberation theologians and which their opponents – from Pope John Paul II to Ronald Reagan, president of the United States – had done much to suppress, the former intellectually and the latter by force of arms. The election of the candidate for change in the Latin American country that was more than any other stamped with the sign of its indigenous past – no indigenous language in the region enjoys the currency that Guaraní does in Paraguay – was also part of a new concern with the cultures of pre-Columbian peoples. In the 1950s, for instance, demands began to be heard for more just treatment from the score of indigenous nations living within the Republic of Guatemala. These were met with revolt and bloodshed enthusiastically backed by foreign governments, from which Guatemala has not yet fully recovered.

But the movement for indigenous rights was not to be suppressed by bayonets and torture chambers. In the twentieth century it continued to manifest itself in domestic politics from the Chiapas region in Mexico

2 Lugo taking oath of office, Asunción, 15 August 2008.

in 1994 to Ecuador, Peru, Bolivia and Chile. Once in office, Lugo strengthened his links with President Evo Morales in La Paz, who came to power on a platform of fairer conditions for the indigenous peoples of the Andes. The prospects for tens of millions of native peoples – and the poor of all races – began to look brighter.

The festivities that surrounded the inauguration of Lugo said much about his plans for the future as he prepared to execute them.

Few enough presidents in Latin America have taken up office in their shirtsleeves without a tie; many have tried to give the impression of being more familiar with the starchy protocol of European aristocracy or the military or naval academies such as Saint-Cyr or Sandhurst than with the lives of their fellow citizens. Lugo decided to take up his presidency in a dazzling white traditional shirt, the *ao po'i*, and grey trousers secured by a black leather belt. To the scandalized cries of a few he even dared to wear sandals. The message was obvious – the formalities of a past age had been superseded.

He was not alone in his informal style of dress. President Evo Morales of neighbouring Bolivia was also without a suit or tie but was in the rich ceremonial dress of his race, the Aymara of the Andean highlands. (The last time Morales had been seen in a suit and tie, they said, had been in 1977 when he posed for the photograph taken when he received his school-leaving certificate. On his world tour after his electoral victory in December 2005, the Bolivian had visited royalty and presidents wearing a woolly jumper.) A third head of state, President Rafael Correa of Ecuador, also dispensed with orthodox formalities of dress. He arrived with his good-looking wife, also without a tie, but with a well-cut jacket covering his colourfully embroidered shirt. President Hugo Chávez had a bright blue tie on some of the time, but he also dispensed with it at other times, opening a khaki shirt to reveal a red vest.

Sitting near Michelle Bachelet of Chile and Cristina Kirchner of Argentina, Lula, the president of Brazil whose supposedly anti-capitalist political programme and subsequent electoral victory in the 2002 elections had pitched the readers of the *Wall Street Journal* into such gloom, looked a model of sartorial orthodoxy in a dark suit and a sober blue-and-white tie. Only the shortened finger, the tip of which he left under a steel press in the São Paulo factory where he had worked, gave a clue to his former existence as the hero of hundreds of thousands of Brazilian industrial workers.

Prominent among the guests in shirtsleeves and a beret was the octogenarian Ernesto Cardenal, the priest-poet of liberation theology and the government minister whom Pope John Paul II made famous worldwide by shaking his finger at him in reproof on his arrival in Managua in 1983 as the Nicaraguan knelt before him. Also there was Leonardo Boff, the liberation theologian from Brazil. Through their years of teaching and pressure for reform in the Church, Boff and Cardenal had provided the new leader with much religious inspiration. Also invited was the Uruguayan left-wing writer Eduardo Galeano, who took the opportunity of apologizing to Lugo, a man with a passion for history, for Uruguay's part in the nineteenth-century War of the Triple Alliance, when his country, Brazil and Argentina attacked their eager and headstrong Paraguayan neighbours.

Prominent among the absentee heads of state were President Álvaro Uribe of Colombia, Washington's main ally in Latin America, and President Alan García of Peru, once the fire-breathing foe of international banks, now the champion of foreign investors and increasingly unpopular with voters in his own country.

Lugo delivered his inaugural speech, one part in the Guaraní of the majority of his fellow citizens, the other part in Spanish. 'Today', he declared, 'marks the end of an exclusive Paraguay, a Paraguay of secrets, a Paraguay known for its corruption; today is the start of a Paraguay whose government and whose citizens will have no truck with those who steal from the people, with actions which cloud over transparency in public life and with those few feudal lords of a strange country of yesteryear which has somehow survived to the present day.'

Distinguished guests came in their hundreds. Ricardo Lagos, the former president of Chile, was also among the many notables, as was Joseph Stiglitz, Nobel Prize winner and once the chief economist at the World Bank. Stiglitz, now one of the Bank's fiercest critics, had delivered a hard-hitting lecture on development economics the previous day in Asunción.

The swearing-in ceremony was followed by a quick visit to a leper colony and a gathering to commemorate the fourth anniversary of the fire in which hundreds died and hundreds more were injured when the owners locked them inside the Ycuá Bolaños supermarket lest they neglect to pay for the goods they were buying. At the party afterwards Lugo and Chávez took the stage to croon suitable songs of protest.

A NON-EXISTENT STATE

The tasks that faced Lugo as he took over on 20 August were immense, since Stroessner after his thirty-six-year dictatorship and the Colorados and their sixty-one-year regime had left Paraguay like a house stricken with dry rot. Behind the mirage of decency – supposedly free elections in a supposed democracy; a supposed system of justice; a supposed respect for people's human and economic rights; a claim to be part of the supposed 'free world'; a supposed respect for minorities and indigenous peoples – there lay advanced decay. According to the UN Development Programme's Human Development Index, which measures life expectancy, education and purchasing power, Paraguay stood in 98th place on a list of 179 countries. If Lugo wanted to carry out the necessary changes he had to have very good plans.

As he prepared to take on the Herculean task of reconstructing Paraguay's economy after the six decades of maladministration and pillage by the Colorados, two of Lugo's main sources of economic advice were Borda, his choice for economy minister, and Joseph Stiglitz, the economist from the World Bank. Borda had, from 2003 to 2005, been finance minister to Nicanor Duarte, from whom Lugo was accepting the presidency. Duarte was the last of an unbroken chain of eleven consecutive presidents from the Colorado party.

Borda's strategy was based on the initial priority of bringing the country into line with most others in the world by curing the gravest deficiency of the state, the chronic lack of money which prevented it from undertaking the most rudimentary tasks of any state.

The first job, Borda commented in June 2008, was the establishment of a professional civil service, hitherto lacking in Paraguay, which would have the capacity to execute the government's policies and which would be out of the reach of political manipulation. That would demand some coherence in the levels of reward civil servants and public sector employees in general could expect in return. 'What we've got now is a real chaos,' he commented, with individuals answering not to the interests of the state but to political interests.

Second, greater professionalism was needed in a situation where those with responsibility had little managerial experience and where there was no coordination among government bodies – with the exception of that between the Finance Ministry and the Central Bank. There was no National Investment Plan, no National Infrastructure Plan, and the lack of tax revenue to construct basic infrastructure, combined with Paraguay's position as a landlocked country, was a serious drag on economic growth. Of Paraguay's 30,000 kilometres of road, for instance, only 5,000 kilometres were surfaced and capable of being used in all weather.

The third job was to define the responsibilities of government servants, who were grouped into 'a great archipelago' of various bodies with overlapping jurisdictions – no fewer than ten ministries and beside them fourteen secretariats with their own responsibilities.

Other government activities had to be put in order, particularly those of the state and regulatory agencies. Three big state concerns, water, electricity and telecommunications, and the oil and cement monopolies were to some extent or other unable to supply the services that the economy wanted from them, or were subject to financial millstones. All these had to be subject to the government regulating their prices and the quality of their services within a framework of a 'public–private partnership'.

The economy had moreover to be made more productive and diversified away from its over-dependence on the production of soya beans and meat. In 2007 the economy grew by 6.8 per cent, 4 per cent from soya and meat and 2.8 per cent from other sectors. Yet it was not providing the jobs that Paraguayans needed. While production went up poverty was growing as well. In 2007 the number of those in extreme poverty increased from 18 to 20 per cent of the population. Agriculture had to provide better-paying jobs with the expansion of agricultural industries. Paraguay's great potential for growing crops, including sunflowers to produce oil and cotton to employ spinners, weavers and makers of garments, had to be promoted. The country had the potential to produce fruit and vegetables in abundance for the juices and sauces that were already starting to be exported, and could produce much greater quantities of maize, wheat, oats, rye and other cereals than it currently did. There could be tea, sesame and plants for medicinal use among many other promising crops.

It was essential in this context to reform the system of justice: investment would not come where investors felt that they were not going to be treated in accordance with the law. At the same time masses of unskilled workers, who had on average less than eight years of schooling – one of the lowest levels in Latin America – had to be given the skills that would enable them to improve themselves. The banking system, which had become used to providing loans for the friends of political leaders, had to turn its attention to the needs of small and medium-sized businesses in a country where most agricultural workers worked on farms of fewer than 50 hectares and most city workers worked in firms with fewer than fifty employees.

The farm sector, Borda said, generated more than a quarter of Paraguay's wealth, gave work to more than a third of the active population and brought in 90 per cent of foreign earnings.

Underlying all this was the need to tackle poverty, given that 1.2 million Paraguayans lived in conditions of extreme poverty with barely enough money to feed themselves. And extreme poverty would not be solved just with economic growth; the government would have to do what it could to provide new jobs in schemes such as road building, which would give a boost to the trade of those running the quarries that produced the country's great variety of useful stone.

One of the government's first policies favoured by Borda, similar to those carried out by Morales in Bolivia and Lula in Brazil, was to increase from 50,000 to 70,000 the number of poor families benefiting from the conditional grant programme. Under this, families were to receive 180,000 guaranies (US$40) a month while their children were kept in school.

Agrarian reform, as Lugo had said, was absolutely essential in a country of amazing inequality, where the richest 10 per cent had forty times the income of the poorest 10 per cent of the population. While the richest 1 per cent of landowners were sitting on 80 per cent of the land, the vast majority of farmers had no more than 1 per cent.

Borda commented that when he was accompanying Lugo on a visit to Spain in 2006 they met José Luis Rodríguez Zapatero, the Spanish prime minister, and fell to discussing economics. When the Spaniard learnt that the state's income from taxation was a mere 12 per cent of the gross national product – compared to three times that proportion in most developed countries – he exclaimed, 'Well, Paraguay as a state doesn't exist, then!'

Once in office Borda was the target of complaints from fellow ministers about his unwillingness to give them funds. The agriculture minister, for instance, announced that he had resigned as he had no money for the seeds that farmers were expecting from him, but that the president had rejected his resignation and told him to get back to work.

For his part, Stiglitz, the other economic adviser, was critical of the increasingly contested Washington Consensus, the ark of the covenant of orthodox thinking in the western hemisphere, which advocated unswerving adherence to markets despite the harm such a policy would do to social structures. By contrast he defended the role of the state in the redistribution of income and promotion of growth in a way that infuriated those who considered themselves guardians of right-thinking Western financial capitals and universities.

His address, delivered in the giant auditorium of the Central Bank of Paraguay to the country's business elite on the eve of Lugo's inauguration, created a great stir – as Lugo expected it would – and it reminded some of Paraguay's most conservative leaders that their opposition to personal taxation and measures to redistribute income was rejected by one of the world's leading economists, a Nobel Prize winner and veteran of the World Bank.

Reform would lead to a growth of the knowledge economy, a closing of the technology gap and an expansion of research at the universities, Stiglitz said. The first need was to expand its tax base so the state could have the funds needed for public investment. Echoing the arguments of Borda, he repeated that the country had to increase the tiny share of the national income going to the state, and that could not be done by a mere exercise in tackling tax evasion. Taxing the country's exporters of beef and soya beans would not be difficult, given that these passed through a relatively few choke points where the taxmen could be stationed. Stiglitz pointed out that neither beef production nor the cultivation of soya were providing enough jobs and were not helping the problem created by the concentration of land in the hands of large landowners to the detriment of the landless – a point that Lugo had been insisting on for years. Agrarian reform, he declared, was a priority. Such an attitude was a shower of cold water on those educated in the Colorado belief that such policies were the purest Castro-communism. Again he echoed Borda in calling for urgent reform of a dilapidated civil service, the promotion of competitive entry and the destruction of the 'jobs for the boys' ethos that had been the norm in Paraguay.

As had been the case with his predecessors, Lugo's prospects for achieving the targets he had set himself for his presidency did not look bad. The trade balance of a country that was among the world's largest producers of soya and other foods, from beef to maize, looked healthy. Foreign reserves were growing. If Lugo could attain his stated objective of doubling the price paid by the Brazilians and the Argentines for the electric power they took from the large jointly run Itaipú and Yacyretá hydroelectric schemes, Paraguay would financially be in clover. Even a much smaller increase in the price paid by those two countries would offer the Paraguayan economy great benefits. Meanwhile many maintained the hope that oil or gas would eventually be discovered.

THE FIRST CHALLENGE

Despite such favourable long-term prospects, on 1 September, within days of his inauguration, the continuing precariousness of the country's politics was made manifest and the new president had to act swiftly and with determination to preserve his presidency. He thought it wise to call together his senior officers to join him as he announced to the country from the presidential palace that 'anti-democratic and retrograde sectors' were harbouring the intention of overthrowing his government by force. The previous evening the former general Lino Oviedo, a turbulent figure with political pretensions, he said, had summoned General Máximo Díaz Cáceres, the officer charged with the job of liaising between the armed forces and the congress, to his house. There Díaz found a group of the president's bitterest political opponents, including ex-president Duarte, Lugo's predecessor, the head of the electoral tribunal and the public prosecutor.

Díaz was questioned about the attitude of the armed forces towards the 'parliamentary crisis'. Unfortunately for Oviedo, Díaz lost no time in telling the president of this. From Brasília, Lula immediately condemned Oviedo's action and pledged Brazil's support for Lugo. Lugo's journey to the United Nations General Assembly on 25 September gave him the opportunity of telling the world of his worries about a military coup. Repeating the message that 'it is not possible to sustain democracy when the great majority is excluded from economic benefits', he said that 'mafias with excessive wealth' had become a threat and that he would not allow the popular will to be challenged. There would be no tolerance for any attempt at destabilization from such people. Less than two months later he replaced the head of the army with the navy commander as chief, under the presidency, of the armed forces. The Asunción press said that Lugo was looking for someone utterly reliable for such a sensitive post. The president's worries about the armed forces and the danger of a military coup had clearly not been wiped away entirely.

As 2009 dawned economic prospects continued to appear favourable, despite financial chaos in Wall Street and the City of London. Though Paraguayans had bitter historical memories of Brazil's role in the War of the Triple Alliance of the 1860s and Brazilian action in the twentieth century in buying up large tracts of eastern Paraguay, the country benefited from the growing international standing of its large neighbour to the east. President Lula certainly gave signs of understanding Paraguay's problems, while his drive for regional integration offered Lugo the prospect of getting access to Brazil's large markets for its exports and an expanding clientele for Paraguay's underdeveloped tourist industry.

Within days of assuming office in August 2008, Lugo made a significant appointment to his cabinet, naming Margarita Mbywangi, a forty-three-year-old mother of three, as minister of indigenous affairs. Her appointment underlined one of the problems facing the new leader: the issue of the indigenous population had to be tackled urgently, but where were the competent people who could do so? The new minister seemed ideal. She was not just a senior figure among the Aché people; she had been a slave, having been seized from her home in the forest and put to forced work before she was ten years old. Yet she was not destined to last long, being dismissed by Lugo before Christmas after complaints about her competence from among her own people and the death of an indigene who was poisoned after eating seed provided by a state organization for which she was responsible.

The week of her appointment was notable because an important development in indigenous affairs in Peru underlined the widespread nature of native peoples' calls for justice throughout Latin America. After a sustained campaign by various native people, who were able to bring to a halt communications in Amazonia, President Alan García of Peru was forced to rescind the latest of a long series of measures that had given concessions to business while whittling away indigenous rights over ancestral lands.

Consequently, indigenous peoples were also active over some of the most prominent scandals in Peru's mining industry. Despite his eagerness for Peru to overtake Chile, its historic rival to the south, in a race to attract the maximum foreign investment, García was under pressure to take account of indigenous rights.

As demonstrated by the cases of Río Blanco, a big new copper mining scheme in the Andes on the border with Ecuador, and La Oroya, a lead refinery bought by a US investor in the central Andes, which continued a shameful story of atmospheric pollution, the rights of the locals on land sought by mining companies counted for little, especially if they were indigenes.

At the same time Lugo, Correa and Morales, all reformists, clearly shared an interest in improving the lot of their indigenous peoples, and were thus in harmony on a question that was becoming more pressing up and down the continent.

FOREIGN RIVALS OR PARTNERS IN UNITY?

Before Christmas 2008 Lugo found himself with Morales and the Cuban vice-president José Fernández in the Bolivian city of Cochabamba, where he announced that Paraguay would adopt the literacy system designed by Cuban educationists and largely paid for with Venezuelan money. Its introduction had allowed Bolivia to claim at the end of 2008 that illiteracy had been eliminated there. The year 2009, Lugo said, would bring 180,000 Paraguayans into the system called *Yo, sí puedo* (Yes, I can), which used *teleclases*, a series of programmes prepared for television and viewed on sets provided in each learning centre.

Making tacit acknowledgement of the campaign of his domestic political opponents against a scheme that they claimed would pull Paraguay into the Cuban and Venezuelan orbit, he argued that it was not a new departure for his country since it had been in use in many departments of Paraguay since 2003, when Fidel Castro gave sixty-five *teleclases* kits to Roa Bastos, the Paraguayan intellectual who was best known internationally, during his visit to Havana.

The Cochabamba meeting suited the political ends of the three participants, all of whom appeared in native dress. Fernández could harvest some credit for Cuba's intellectual authorship of the classes. Morales could be seen to be bringing distinguished foreign visitors to an important Bolivian provincial city, where anti-government forces were strong and often violent. The meeting would also show that the Bolivian president had the authority to bolster Cochabamba's ambitions to become an effective centre of regional influence and reinforce the importance it had already achieved by being chosen as the site of a re-invigorated Latin American parliament. Lugo's presence at Cochabamba undermined opposition claims that he was a new boy in the community of regional leaders and not yet fully accepted by them.

The opposition – notably the Fundación Libertad, a local organization of the far right linked to neoconservatives in the USA and the National Endowment for Democracy (NED), a body financed by the US government and US Congress – echoed the quiet murmurs from the Bush administration that Lugo's was another of these confounded reformist regimes which could not be relied on to support Washington's nationalist agenda in the region.

Both the Fundación Libertad and the NED did their best to pour cold water on Lugo's programme, putting it about that the first hundred days of his administration had resulted in nothing very much. Some Paraguayans suggested that the two organizations were desperately trying to tempt Lugo into some noisy new strategy which Washington could dress up as a leftward lurch towards Castro or Chávez.

There remained Paraguay's relationship with Argentina. This had preoccupied governments in Asunción in the nineteenth and twentieth centuries, when the Argentines exerted control over the rivers. Now, however, Paraguay was gaining greater access to the ocean through Brazil. Paraguayan governments had no great quarrel with their neighbour to the south or with the Kirchners, the husband and wife who succeeded in turn to the Argentine presidency, apart from the question of obtaining better remuneration for the sale of Paraguay's share of the electric power from the Yacyretá hydroelectric scheme. At the same time many humbler Paraguayans found it hard to forget the sort of mistreatment and financial exploitation that many of them had suffered when they emigrated to Argentina in search of employment. (Though it can have offered them little consolation, the president of Bolivia had similar feelings. His indigent parents had taken the young Evo Morales with them when they went to work hard for little pay as agricultural labourers in Argentina.)

As 2008 was coming to an end, Lugo received his first recognition as a leader in the Latin American integration process at the thirty-sixth summit of Mercosur, held at Sauípe in north-eastern Brazil, where he was chosen to succeed Lula as the organization's president pro tem. The gathering was hailed by enthusiasts of regional integration as particularly important as it was held without the presence of representatives of the USA or Canada. The summit meeting signalled the organization's increasing ambitions by creating a fund for small and medium-sized businesses, signing agreements for reductions of tariffs with the countries of southern Africa, and advocating closer relations with Chile. Lugo called for a 'just Mercosur', which would bring peoples and not just governments together and really promote Latin American unity.

2 | AN ISLAND SURROUNDED BY LAND

The events that led to the election of Fernando Lugo, a Catholic bishop who was a champion of the rights of the indigenous peoples, as leader of his country were rooted deep in the history of the indigenes and of the Catholic Church in Paraguay and the continent of America. Remote and difficult to know, wreathed in clouds of legend, Paraguay has seemed to invite, or indeed challenge, people of imagination to represent it to the outside world. For many, it has been difficult to pin down with any geographical accuracy, given its location among the broad and erratic rivers and sandbanks in the watery heart of South America. Paraguay's often imprecise borders seemed to vary puzzlingly in the light of Paraguayans' struggles with their neighbours. For Paraguay's greatest novelist, Augusto Roa Bastos, it was 'an island surrounded by land'.

It is not fanciful to say that the refusal of the Guaranís to bow the knee to Europeans seeking to reduce them to the level of slaves in the decades after the arrival of the Spaniards in 1492 was echoed in the arrangements for the ceremonies surrounding Lugo's assumption of office in Asunción in 2008. As we have seen, part of his first speech as president was delivered in Guaraní, and he was accompanied on the rostrum by two fellow presidents, Morales of Bolivia and Correa of Ecuador, wearing indigenous dress, and a third, Chávez of Venezuela, who would have been embarrassed to have been photographed in the style of dress adopted by a European or US head of state.

The fact that Lugo was able to win the presidency stemmed from the fact that few Paraguayans were without some proportion of indigenous blood. Those voters who were particularly conscious of their ethnic origins and wanted to see the indigenes' lot improved saw in him a person who could reverse the subjection in which they and their predecessors had been living for 500 years.

The decision of Lugo on the day of his investiture as president to address his fellow countrymen in Guaraní as well as Spanish was not a mere political quirk, it was an important symbolic action.

That there were Guaranís not just surviving in the country but also maintaining a culture so strong that no politician aspiring to a position of prominence in Paraguay could afford to ignore them owed much to two factors. The first and more important was their own determination and self-respect. Unlike those of the Tainos in the Caribbean, the language and ways of life of the Guaranís had survived tenaciously. Their traditional social system was of farming families living in villages surrounded by stockades that were moved as agriculture exhausted the surrounding land. There, shamans were revered and kept the communities' historical memory alive.

The Guaraní-Tupy races were to be found in many of the non-mountainous areas of South America. Their culture could not compare in physical grandeur with that of the Andean peoples, such as the Aymaras and Quechuas, founders of an Inca empire that stretched from the modern borders between Ecuador and Colombia to the north of Chile. Like the indigenes on the North American plains they had no stone with which to create structures to rival the pyramids and temples of Mexico and Central America or the fine masonry of Cusco or Machu Picchu. Yet, like the peoples of what is now Brazilian Amazonia, they mastered the potter's techniques. In their wars they practised cannibalism. In his book *Conquista Espritual del Paraguay* (Spiritual Conquest of Paraguay), published in 1639, Antonio Ruiz de Montoya, a Jesuit missionary, relates how they ate the prisoners they captured in war: 'Commonly they share out pieces of this body, from which pieces cooked in much water they make fritters and it is a celebrated feast for those who go in for much ceremony.'

In the matter of language the Guaranís were subtle and sophisticated. The Paraguayan historian Efraín Cardozo quotes Ruiz de Montoya as referring to Guaraní as 'as copious and elegant a language as could with reason compete with famous ones', while another Jesuit, José Manuel Peramás, said in 1793, 'I would never have thought that among barbarians there should exist a language which is no way inferior in my judgement in harmony and nobility to those I learned in another time in Europe.'

In the 1630s Ruiz de Montoya wrote three books that went a long way towards rescuing the language from any danger of obliteration, *Tesoro de la lengua Guaraní* (Treasury of the Guaraní language), *Arte y vocabulario Guaraní* (Guaraní Art and Vocabulary) and *Catecismo de la lengua Guaraní* (Catechism of the Guaraní Language).

The Guaraní word for 'wind', for instance, is *yvytu*, 'the breath of the earth'; 'beautiful', *porã*, means 'like a flower'; while a person's pupil is *tesa ỹ'i*, 'the seed of the eyes'. The language is full of onomatopoeia – 'thunder' is *sununú*, 'waterfall' is *chororó*, the 'fluttering of a bird's wing' is *opepé*, 'the gurgling of a stream' is *syryry*, while *pororó* is 'an explosion'.

In Chapter XXXI of his *Essais*, Michel de Montaigne, the seventeenth-century French essayist, compared the language to Greek, and quoted two poems in Guaraní to strengthen his argument. The first was the cry of defiance by a prisoner about to be killed and eaten by his cannibal captors which ends:

Taste my warm remains; don't fear to savour them
And you will know, at last, the taste of your own flesh.

The second was a love poem.

Stop, snake; snake, stop
So my sister can copy
From your beautiful colours the model
Of a rich belt that I could
Give to my beloved.
And may your beauty always be preferred
To that of all the other snakes.

In Guaraní society poets and poetesses were particularly honoured and their society had *ayé*, wise men and wise women who claimed the power to communicate with the spirits. Without ever forming a priestly caste, they maintained the sense of magic and the power of a supreme being who was creator of all.

The people who generated such a sophisticated society gave signs of being capable of resisting most attempts to snuff them out culturally.

The second factor favouring the survival of Guaraní culture was that ever since the first years of European penetration of the western hemisphere there had been a consciousness among the leaders of the colonizing power – though not among the European rank and file – that they had duties towards the people they colonized. King Ferdinand and Queen Isabella, styled the Catholic Sovereigns, had after all sent Columbus to the New World not just – or even primarily – to find treasure. He also went to spread the gospel. From the very beginning there was a tension between those whose priority was fortune-hunting and those whose first concern was evangelization.

The influence of the Church continued long after Spanish colonial rule was swept away. Though the nineteenth century was a difficult one for the Church, not least because of self-inflicted wounds such as the suppression of the Jesuits, its authority grew in the twentieth.

Writing a decade before Lugo's victory, Ricardo Medina, a prominent

member of the Paraguayan left who in his youth had joined the Paraguayan Communist Party and studied in the Soviet Union, had no
qualms about pointing to the importance of the Catholic Church in
Paraguay as a force for much-needed social reform. Dismissive of much
left-wing activity in his country during the Stroessner era, he wrote,
'Paradoxically, the only voices still sympathetic towards the profoundly
humane content of the socialist ideal came from sectors linked to the
Catholic Church. These defended socialism not in terms of the aborted
Soviet model, but as the creation of a democratic and socially just
society.'

At the same time, throughout the history of Latin America many
in the Church betrayed their ideals. They supported the state and the
wealthy and ignored the needy. Many times over the centuries the
Inquisition gave a greater priority to what its officials considered to be
theological orthodoxy than they did to justice or charity. Up and down
the region the Church disgraced itself. Throughout the cold war in
modern times military chaplains and the special caste of bishops who
were appointed to oversee them acquiesced in human rights violations,
blessing the murderous missions the troops were charged to carry out. In
his book *Doble Juego: la Argentina Católica y Miltar*, whose cover carries
a photograph of the papal nuncio Pío Laghi and another prelate in
animated and clearly cordial conversation with General Videla, Horacio
Verbitsky chronicles the repulsively intimate relations that existed between senior Church figures and the architects of Argentina's Dirty War
of repression, torture and kidnapping.

THE EXAMPLE OF LAS CASAS

Yet the Church, too, produced some admirable and outstanding
figures. Those, like Lugo, who embrace liberation theology trace their
school of thought to the scriptures but also to the man whom they
particularly revere, the towering sixteenth-century figure of Bartolomé
de las Casas. Las Casas devoted his life as a churchman to the welfare
of the native peoples of America who suffered grievously from the
arrival of the Europeans. Speaking in the Ecuadorean city of Guayaquil
in August 2007 at a conference on Twenty-first Century Socialism
attended by President Correa, Lugo mentioned Las Casas specifically
as one of his models. To applause he declared, 'I tell you that I come
from a tradition of Bartolomé de las Casas, of Saint Romero of America
[the murdered archbishop of San Salvador Oscar Romero, much disliked
by conservatives in the Vatican] and of the holy men and women who
gave their lives for the indigenous communities.'

Born, probably in 1474, in Seville, Las Casas saw his father Pedro go off with Christopher Columbus on the latter's second voyage to America in 1493. Rather than the mere eighty-seven men that he had taken on his first venture, the discoverer took 1,200 in 1493 with the idea of founding permanent settlements in Hispaniola, the island now occupied by Haiti and the Dominican Republic. Pedro returned for his son in 1502 and Bartolomé was on hand to see the increasingly bad relations developing between the incomers, avid to recover gold, and the indigenes, whose labour was vital if Spanish dreams were to be realized. Father and son both obtained land near Santo Domingo under the encomienda system, which the Spaniards put together in an unsuccessful attempt to conciliate the interests of God and Mammon. This gave the European colonists – the *encomenderos* – the duty of bringing the indigenes to baptism while at the same time giving the white men the right to put them to work in mines and plantations. This produced much more brutality than baptisms. Indeed, the imposition of the encomienda in the Antilles was so savage that the natives often preferred mass suicide to slavery at the hands of the newcomers.

Las Casas resolved to become a priest and, on his return to Europe, went to Rome in 1506 and was there ordained by dispensation of Pope Julius II the following year.

Back again as a landlord in Hispaniola, Las Casas turned away from the life of a settler and became the chaplain to the Spanish force invading Cuba in 1512. There he was horrified by his compatriots' treatment of the indigenous people, particularly the torturing to death by the Spanish colonists in 1511 of Hatuey, the native leader with a following in Hispaniola and Cuba.

In his history of the conquest, Las Casas wrote that when the Spaniards eventually captured the resister in eastern Cuba they condemned Hatuey to be burnt. As he was being tied to the stake a Franciscan friar called on him to embrace Christianity, which would, the friar said, open the gates of heaven to him. Las Casas recounted that the chieftain replied 'that he did not want to go there but to hell so he would not be with Spaniards, and not see such cruel people'. Las Casas went on to describe how 3,000 Indians had been put to the sword in front of him and how more than 7,000 children had starved because the Spaniards had taken away their fathers and mothers for work in the mines. He repeatedly wrote that the bad treatment meted out by the Spaniards to the indigenes was unchristian and hindered the task of spreading the gospel to them, which they were obliged by the crown of Spain to promote.

From then until his death in Madrid in 1566, Las Casas devoted his life to shuttling across the ocean and lobbying the Spanish monarchy for an end to the abuses of the European colonists. Queen Isabella had decreed in 1500 that the indigenes were her subjects and 'free and not subject to servitude', but the settlers ignored the decree. Las Casas argued the Indians' case at the Spanish court with little success. By 1517 he was back in Santo Domingo and in 1523 joined the Dominican order.

He was offered the grand diocese of Cusco, the former Inca capital in Peru, rejected that, but in 1543 accepted the southernmost diocese of Mexico, Ciudad Real de Chiapas, today renamed San Cristóbal de las Casas, and was consecrated bishop. But after two years he gave it up. He returned to Spain in 1547 in a hurry to seek to prop up the cause of more justice for the indigenes against the attacks of those who were trying to persuade the king to side with the Spanish settlers against his indigenous subjects.

The friar poured out his condemnations of colonialism in various books, notably his *Brevísima relación de la destrucción de las Indias* (Briefest Account of the Destruction of the Indies), a powerful and angry document which he dedicated to Prince Philip, later to succeed to the throne as Philip II of Spain. It made him few friends among his fellow countrymen.

In his *History of the Indies* he wrote:

> From the first hour when I began to dispel that [Spanish] ignorance,
> I never read in a book written in Latin or Spanish ... where there
> were not reason or authority to prove and corroborate the justice of
> these Indian people and to condemn the injustices which have been
> done to them and their bad treatment.

The indefatigable old Dominican, Lugo's ideological mentor, died in Madrid in 1566, and his efforts to defend the Indians against the settlers' colonial system were well summed up by Josep Barnadas in the *Cambridge History of Latin America*:

> He fought it as a secular priest, as a friar and as a bishop, as a coun-
> cillor at court, as a polemicist, as a historian, as a delegate for the
> Indians. He allied himself with the crown to get the settlers' privileges
> annulled; he exerted pressure on the friars' conscience to stop absolu-
> tion to the encomenderos; he propagated his own version of what the
> Indians should be in writing; he prophesied the destruction of Spain
> as its punishment for the cruelties it had inflicted on innocent Indians
> ... he belongs among the greater reformers and 'liberators' in the
> church's history.

Nor was Las Casas's voice a lone one in the region. Bartolomeu Melià, SJ, a prominent modern expert on the Paraguayan indigenes, recalls how, even before the first Jesuit reduction or settlement for native peoples was founded in Paraguay, Martín Ignacio de Loyola, a Franciscan friar, was trenchant about the freedom of the native peoples. With all the authority of one who was a great-nephew of the founder of the Jesuits and fifth bishop of Paraguay between 1601 and 1605, he laid down how the indigenes had to be respected. In instructions to priests hearing the confessions of Spanish settlers or soldiers, he hammered home the idea that the Indians had as much right to freedom as any European. He decreed:

> 4. That those who have brought from their settlements Indian women or boys or girls against the will of their parents, relations or chief (even if they were orphans) are obliged to restore them to their land and their chief.
>
> 5. That the captains and military men who have enforced service from Indian settlements ... the Indians not having committed any offence worthy of such punishment as taking their children and women from them ... that confessors should oblige them to free them from such service ... and satisfy the wrong done to them, by giving them a few items and begging their pardon ...
>
> 7. That those who had benefited from forced labour of Indians over and above that which the Governor had in justice fixed must pay those Indians.

Those who ignored a confessor's instruction in any grave matter, the Church taught, ran the risk of eternal damnation.

In Brazil, Antônio Vieira, one of the most powerful stylists that the Portuguese language ever produced, who arrived in Brazil in 1653 as provincial of the Jesuits, made it his business to tell the settlers and the king in Lisbon exactly what he thought of their conduct towards the indigenous peoples. 'All of you are in mortal sin,' he thundered, 'all of you live in a state of condemnation; and all of you are going directly to hell!'

In Paraguay, the spirit of Las Casas was still alive and inspiring in the twenty-first century.

THE JESUITS AND THEIR REDUCTIONS

Like the Dominicans, the Jesuits intervened early to help the indigenes to organize themselves against their enemies, notably the

3 Lugo with Pope John Paul II at the Vatican, 1978.

slave-hunters pushing in from the Atlantic coasts, keen to hijack labour for the plantations of the Portuguese lands of Brazil. For two centuries the Jesuits helped to shape the Church that Lugo embraced with such commitment. It was to a Jesuit-run university, the Gregorianum in Rome, that Lugo was sent for postgraduate study, and where his eyes were opened to the realities of the Vatican, Europe and the wider world.

The first three Jesuits arrived in 1587. The first reduction for the indigenes was established in 1609 by two Jesuits at Loreto on the Paraná river, near which, over the next twenty years, ten more were established with a total population of 40,000 or more. Their efforts to spread Christianity, according to the Jesuits, included the incorporation into the evangelization process of many concepts known to the Guaraní. They acknowledged a spirit called Ñamandú, who existed before the sun was born. They believed that the earth was supported by crossed sticks. They sought what the Spaniards termed the *Tierra sin males*, the land without evil, which could be found somewhere on the planet. There, crops would grow by themselves and those who successfully sought it would be able to enter and live at their ease. These concepts were seen by the missionaries as cognate with Christian notions of God the Father, Jesus's cross and heaven.

The Jesuits gathered together Guaraní Indians who were thankful to find relief from the Europeans who had arrived in the region a century previously. The Spaniards, having been given land granted by the Spanish crown, were eager to use the indigenes as cheap labour; Portuguese gangs, called *bandeirantes* or flagmen, regularly came over the border from Brazil to the east hunting for slaves whom they could drag back to their own plantations. With royal permission from the king of Spain, the Jesuits were the organizers of the fast-expanding settlements, and the artificers of the armed militia, which kept stocks of firearms and ammunition, defended the indigenes from marauders, European and local alike. The example that the Jesuits set in defending the indigenous people was one that Lugo constantly made clear he wanted to imitate.

European visitors, possible bearers of illnesses against which the indigenes had little protection, were discouraged on the Jesuit reductions, though not banned outright. Yet the fathers respected the indigenous leaders; they themselves were so few in number in relation to the Guaraní – often no more than two in a reduction – that there would have been no alternative even if they had wanted one.

Philip Caraman, the scholarly English Jesuit who in the twentieth century produced *Lost Paradise*, the best history of the settlements in English, reports a contemporary account of life in the reductions.

> Their churches were more stately and better adorned than any in
> Tucumán or Paraguay. They had trained choirs of musicians that
> differed little from those in Europe ... Each house had its own patio in
> the rear in which hens, geese and flocks of domestic birds were kept.
> The fields produced cereals and cotton, so that the Indians carried on
> a real trade in their cloth and at the same time provided clothing for
> all naked travellers, Indian and European. Flocks of sheep and goats
> could be seen in the fields and herds of cattle and mules in the lowland
> pastures which were intersected by rivers that abounded in fish.

As he grew up in his parents' house in the southern city of Encarnación, Lugo was constantly made aware of the Jesuits' work in Paraguay. Just outside Encarnación lay the ruins of the reduction of Trinidad, which boasted the stateliest and best adorned of all the reduction churches, and, a few miles farther on, the remains of the reduction of Jesús. In his youth, as today, Trinidad was appreciated and admired as one of the country's most outstanding historical monuments.

Its architects were Juan Bautista Primoli of Milan and José Grimau, a Catalan, both Jesuit brothers. One visitor who came just after the expulsion of the Jesuits from the lands of the king of Spain in 1767 said, 'Had it been finished it would have been peerless throughout America and very enviable even in the principal cities of Europe.' Trinidad, with its influences of Portuguese Manueline architecture and the styles of the Spanish brothers Churriguera, was a constant reminder to the young Fernando and all the city's inhabitants, the Encarnacenos, of what had been the glories of Paraguay's Church.

In 1901 R. B. Cunninghame Graham produced his book *A Vanished Arcadia*. Writing of the actions of some clergy in protecting the Guaraní, he trenchantly declared:

That the Jesuits rendered the Indians happy is certain … All that I know is myself, in the deserted missions, five-and-twenty years ago I often have met old men who spoke regretfully of Jesuit times, who cherished all the customs left by the Company, and though they spoke at secondhand, repeating but the stories they had heard in youth, kept the illusion that the missions in the Jesuits' time had been a paradise.

For his part, Philip Caraman remarked:

In the sense that both the public and the private life of the Indians was ruled by religion it can be claimed that the Reductions formed the only theocratic commonwealth in Christian history. The inspiration did not come, as is sometimes said, from any preconceived notion of an ideal state after the pattern of St Thomas More's Utopia or the Christian communist community outlined in the City of the Sun by the Dominican Campanella.

What the reductions did, Caraman decided, was to free the indigenes from the horrors of rule by the Europeans, which led to their oppression and consequent deep aversion for the religion of their oppressors. The new settlements thereby encouraged them to accept the gospel. The Jesuits went about their mission with grace and style, as the history of their music and sculpture shows. For instance, among the Jesuits who came to the region was a man who was undoubtedly America's foremost musician in the eighteenth century. A Tuscan, Domenico Zipoli, once apprenticed to Alessandro Scarlatti in Naples, joined the Society and settled in Córdoba, where he produced a great deal of music for the reductions, some of which must still lie undiscovered. He died of tuberculosis in the city in 1726 before he could be ordained a priest.

In the museum of Santa María de Fe, one of the most notable reductions, are more than forty statues, carved, gilded and painted in local cedar in the seventeenth and eighteenth centuries, the sole survivors of the hundreds that adorned the original mission church and which have since been destroyed. They took the eye of curators in Europe, who sought to borrow some of the most magnificent examples of baroque art to have been created in America temporarily for exhibitions. But the curators dreamt in vain. When the villagers learned of the plans they camped outside the door. 'We had all the paperwork ready for the temporary loan of four to French museums but the parishioners stopped that. I had to present excuses to the French ambassador,' said Isabelino Martínez, who was looking after the collection in 2008.

Whatever the reductions were, whatever shelter they had given to the Guaranís, they were swept into oblivion late in the eighteenth century. A combination of jealousy mixed with no little *odium theologicum* among other church organizations, particularly the Jansenists in France, and the deistic philosophy of the age, which held that there was a supreme being but one that did not worry itself too much about mortals, fuelled the anti-Jesuit feeling. They were banished from Portugal and its colony Brazil in 1759 and from France in 1764. In Madrid, the capital of empire, rumours abounded that the Jesuits were planning to seize power in the Paraguayan colony from the king's representative with the aid of the militias, at the time the largest standing military force in South America, whom the Jesuits had trained for the defence of the reductions. Charles III became convinced that the Jesuits in Spain were planning to dethrone him and replace him with his brother. It was further whispered to him mendaciously that they were preparing to announce that he was illegitimate and were prepared to back his assassination. None of this was true, but that did not stop him decreeing the dissolution of the order in his lands.

Despite the arguments of their supporters, were their determined opponents in the courts of Europe right to say these clever people of the Company of Jesus were throwing a veil over a marvellous but remote money-making enterprise, which would fill their order's coffers in the Old World? Was Charles right in issuing the decree, in which the justifications for his action were kept suspiciously vague? Signing it at the Pardo palace on 27 February 1767, he proclaimed:

> urged on by the gravest reasons, pertaining to the obligations incumbent upon me to keep my peoples in subordination, peace and justice and other urgent, just and necessary ones which I reserve

to my royal self: availing myself of the supreme economic authority
which the Almighty has placed in my hands for the protection of
my vassals and respect for my crown: I have decided to order the
exile from my dominions in Spain and the Indies, the Philippines
and other adjacent islands of the religious of the Company, priests,
helpers or laymen who have made their first profession and novices
who desire to follow them and who have to do with all the temporal
affairs of the Company in my dominions ...

On 21 July 1773 the end came for the Jesuits, who were dissolved
by Rome for forty-one years. Clement XIV issued a brief *Dominus
ac Redemptor Noster*, which bore some parallels with Charles III's
decree, and which concluded: 'For the sake of peace, and because
the Society can no longer attain the aims for which it was founded,
and on secret grounds which we enclose in our heart, we suppress
the said Society.'

. On 3 July 1767 the Jesuits in Asunción, offering no opposition to the
king's command, were rounded up for transportation back to Europe (no
Jesuits were Guaranís). Their departure was one of the most important
events in Paraguay's history. They numbered about four hundred, of
whom three hundred were priests. (In 1759 the worldwide tally of Jesuit
priests, excluding brothers, came to 11,293; the similar figure for 2007
was 13,486 priests.)

A year passed before new clergy could be found to replace those on
the reductions, but by July 1770 all the many scores of them had been
expelled. The only exception was Father Sigismund Aperger from Inns-
bruck, the bedridden herbalist and physician known as the Hippocrates
of South America, who was to survive alone for another ten years before
his death at the reduction of Apóstoles at the age of ninety-one. The
expelled men were allowed to take all their possessions. These did not
bespeak great wealth. Father Pedro Zabaleta, whose case was typical, left
with ten shirts, two pillowcases, two sheets, two pocket handkerchiefs,
two pairs of shoes, two pairs of socks and, his only indulgence, a pound
and a half of snuff. The clothes and the snuff came from a stock common
to them all. The reductions fell into decay, their stock animals ran wild
(an inventory of Jesuit goods taken at the time of their expulsion talked
of 719,761 cattle, 44,183 oxen, 27,204 horses and 138,827 sheep). The
fruit trees were cut down for firewood and the *yerba mate* plantations
decayed. Many of Zipoli's scores were lost. The indigenes faced a late-
eighteenth-century colonial society with no friends at court.

The judgement about the reductions written in 1780 by Voltaire, not a man partial to the religion of Rome or to the Jesuits after he left the school where they educated him, is surprising in its fulsomeness:

> When in 1768 the missions of Paraguay left the hands of the Jesuits, they had arrived at perhaps the highest degree of civilization to which it is possible to conduct a young people, and certainly at a far superior state than that which existed in the rest of the new hemisphere. The laws were respected there, morals were pure, a happy brotherhood united every heart, all the useful arts were in a flourishing state, and even some of the more agreeable sciences; plenty was universal.

In creating their reductions the Jesuits left an indelible mark on Paraguay's history and by their actions saved the Guaraní from the enslavement and Guaraní culture from the oblivion which overtook other indigenous people in the western hemisphere. From the ruins of Trinidad near his home in Paraguay to the lecture halls of their university in Rome they also left an indelible mark on Lugo. His policies and actions as he sought political power illustrated the extent to which he sought to protect the most vulnerable in Paraguayan society.

FRANCIA LIVES

Those who expected all Lugo's inspiration to be derived from the Church were in for a surprise when they listened to the speech he delivered immediately after he had been sworn in as president that day in August 2008. The first historical reference he made in it was to a man whose life would have been a closed book to many of the foreign visitors, but whose career as a theologian-turned-politician Lugo was already emulating. That did not stop the brand-new president exclaiming with rapturous emotion: 'In every millimetre of our being boils up challenge: the reconstruction of the dream of José Gaspar Rodríguez de Francia, out of the merit of solidarity, social equity and the identity which embraces us.' This was a man whom the new president clearly valued.

Later that day Lugo enquired whether there was a portrait of Francia in the Palacio de López, the presidential office. When he was told there was not he announced he would be installing one. The new president's announcement was also a gift to Paraguayans who thought they detected a certain authoritarianism in a man whom some got into the habit of calling – privately of course – 'the Ayatollah'.

Francia was the enigmatic figure who instructed his fellow country-men in the skills of being loyal Paraguayans. Born in 1766 in Asunción to an artillery captain of Portuguese origin serving in the Spanish army and his Paraguayan wife, he learnt grammar and Latin with the

Dominicans and the Franciscans in their schools in Asunción and went off to university in Córdoba, now in Argentina. He returned home with a doctorate in theology in 1785, but quit the clerical life and went to help on his father's tobacco plantation. He participated in the triumvirate that in 1811 declared Paraguay free of rule from Spain, and for the next twenty-nine years he dominated Paraguayan politics by fear and force, passionate to keep the Argentines at arm's length and raging at the power they had to throttle Paraguay through their hold on its access to the Atlantic. A Scots businessman who met him in 1812, John Parish Robertson, wrote of him in terms which, eerily, could be applied nearly two centuries later to a large extent to Lugo himself:

> He encouraged the aspirations of men who had hitherto never dreamt of obtaining power; he was all meekness and condescension to the lower, all hauteur to the higher classes of society. His plan was to imbue the country-people with a feeling that they were misgoverned by a few ignorant men devoid of merit, and to insinuate that if he should one day come back into power how different it would be ...

The General Congress, formed by the tiny group of respectable men in the post-colonial society, resolved on 1 June 1816 as follows: 'Noting the full confidence citizen José Gaspar de Francia has justly obtained from the people he is declared and established Perpetual Dictator of the Republic while he lives.'

From then until his death in 1840 tales came out from Asunción of El Supremo, who fixed his country in a cocoon of steel, allowing few people in or out, naming himself the head of the Church and using terror where necessary to impose his will on his countrymen in a not unsuccessful attempt to forge some sort of national identity. The only port that was entitled to trade with a neighbouring country was Itapúa, later to be known as Encarnación and destined to be Lugo's home for most of the first two decades of his life. The action of this haughty, withdrawn bachelor, often to be seen with a cup of *yerba mate* and a cigar, often increased the sense of mystery about the country, but Francia certainly became an icon for the Paraguayan left because of his resistance to the emergence of large landowners and the maintenance of land in the hands of the state and of small farmers.

Inheriting from Spain that half of the country which were crown lands, and taking over the lands of the exiled Jesuits and the remaining religious orders, Francia set up state farms, the *estancias de la patria* (estates of the fatherland), or let out land to small producers. He diversified agriculture, setting production quotas for all crops from tobacco and sugar to cotton and hides, while also fostering the breeding of horses, mules and cattle.

A CENTURY OF CHAOS AND TRAGEDY

Francia's death was followed by a century on which Lugo has looked back with little enthusiasm, embracing as it did two terrible wars and a period of political hopelessness in the middle, which seemed to prove that the Paraguayans were incapable of governing themselves.

In 1844 Carlos Antonio López, the son of a tailor, was elected president for ten years, though he stayed a good deal longer. He did much to modernize the country, bringing the first railway and a Victorian-styled railway station, and a theatre modelled on La Scala in Milan, to the capital and introducing the waltz and the minuet and evening dress into high society. He also brought a steelworks, where Paraguay could produce its own cannon for the first time. He finally got the Argentine authorities grudgingly to admit that Paraguay was independent and not a semi-detached province of Argentina.

He was followed in 1862 by his ambitious son, the short, fat, be-medalled dictator Francisco Solano López, with his dashing Irish mistress, Eliza Lynch, a divorcee from Cork whom he had picked up in the dazzling salons of Paris. The younger López set about invading Brazil and attacking another two neighbours, Argentina and Uruguay, in what became known as the War of the Triple Alliance. The Paraguayans, or at least their leaders, relying on the high technology that their English and Scottish armourers had brought them, were confident of victory. Their confidence was as strong as it was misplaced. In 1863 and 1865, as hostilities began to engulf the country, López saw that the Catechism of San Alberto was reissued in Asunción. (The work of a bishop of Tucumán, Josephantonio de San Alberto, the Catechism was originally conceived as a defence of the traditional view of the Divine Right of Kings and a blast against the indigenes under José Gabriel Condorcanqui, alias Tupac Amaru.)

In the end the Paraguayan leader, with his teenage son Panchito, already a general, was surrounded and butchered by the Brazilian cavalry as the beautiful Eliza looked on sorrowing. In the minds of his supporters, romance, nobility, bravery, glamour and patriotism shone from the scene of his death in 1870 at the skirmish at Cerro Corá, far away to the north-east of Asunción and distant from the battlefields of the south, where his forces had kept the armies of the three powers at bay longer than any observer had ever thought possible.

The most potent observer of the war was a young Argentine *primitif* painter, Cándido López, born in Buenos Aires in 1840. He lost his right arm during the fighting but completed his depictions of the battlefields with his left hand. They show the tented quarters of infantry and cavalry of all armies on the broad empty plains of Paraguay, the dead and dying in the trenches and in the bogs of the battlefields as men struggled across pontoons or forded rivers with the cattle which were later to be their food. López elegantly captures the particular butchery of the battle of Curupaity, where the two sides battled for the 2-kilometre-long trench 2 metres deep and 3 metres wide behind which the Paraguayans vainly sought to halt the advance of the 18,000 enemy soldiers on land and their navies on the broad Paraguay river.

The Batería Londres, the artillery emplacement at Humaitá a kilometre or two north of Curupaity on the Paraguay river and named after the British experts who had done so much to improve Paraguayan military technology, fell into abandonment and remained so until the twenty-first century. (The Paraguayans might not have been so keen on the name London if they had realized at the time that Queen Victoria's ministers were quietly assisting the Triple Alliance.) But Paraguayans remember how for many months it and the soldiers who manned it kept a powerful Brazilian fleet at a prudent distance and stopped them sailing upstream to capture Asunción. Beside the battery stand the preserved ruins of the town's church, which was shelled to bits by the Brazilian warships.

By the time of his defeat and death, López's original army of 100,000 was reduced to very little. The Argentine leader, Domingo Faustino Sarmiento, exulted at the end of the war that no Paraguayan male between ten and fifty years of age was left alive.

The vanquished had to lament the loss of tens – even perhaps hundreds – of thousands of Paraguayan lives, the ruination of the economy and a decade of foreign military occupation.

The war hit the clergy hard. At the beginning, in 1865, there were a little more than a hundred priests in the country. The dictator López shot twenty-four, including the archbishop, seventeen died on the battlefield and thirty-nine just disappeared. Of the thirty-three remaining, eight were made prisoners of war in the final battle of Cerro Corá.

There was also the imposition of a huge indemnity payable to the victors, which continued to be claimed by the Brazilians until the time of the Second World War. A fierce opponent of López put it succinctly half a century after the end of the war: 'We swear eternal hatred of Marshal Francisco Solano López but we venerate the memory of his glorious soldiers.'

At the beginning of the last century Paraguayan politics were justifiably seen as so much posturing by clans who differed little in their strategies but who were not averse to spilling blood in order to protect them. Two parties both founded within weeks of each other in 1887, the ANR (the National Republican Association) or Colorados (Reds) and the Liberals, battled it out. The Colorados clung to traditional values; the Liberals, in whose minds Freemasonry had taken root, were vaguely committed to less Church influence in society. Both were establishment-minded and socially conservative. In practical politics both were riven by splits and rivalries and moved by the wishes of whichever personality had control of the party. The Colorados were in power until 1904 and the Liberals for the following forty years.

TWO YEARS: FIVE PRESIDENTS

The precariousness of politics was well illustrated by the events around 1911. On the first day of that year, for example, Manuel Gondra was in the middle of a presidential period that was to last all of two months. He had got to the presidency on the whim of Colonel Albino Jara, a merciless soldier who had rejoiced in the brutality of the politics of the day, which saw opponents killing, imprisoning or exiling one another and filling the diplomatic missions in Asunción with those seeking asylum from the chaos on the streets. On 11 January Gondra was ousted by Jara, whom he had earlier named his minister of war. Jara himself lasted until 5 June, when he was overthrown by his own supporters. Attired in white tie and tails in the dinghy that was about to take him to the ship in the Bay of Asunción waiting to bear him into exile in Buenos Aires, the gallant Colonel shouted, 'Ungrateful people who call me a tyrant!'

On 5 July Congress designated Liberato Marcial Rojas provisional president. He was subjected to a *mauvais quart d'heure* on 14 January 1912, when a Revolutionary Committee lead by Lieutenant Colonel Alfredo Aponte overthrew him. Rojas resigned and boarded the *Tymbirá*, a Brazilian vessel in the harbour, which took him downstream to the Argentine port of Corrientes. The Revolutionary Committee, or Triumvirate, meanwhile appointed Deputy Ricardo Brugada, a leader of the Colorados, with full presidential powers. But that was not the end of it; 200 died in factional battles in the streets of Asunción. On 17 January Rojas decided to cancel his resignation and return from Corrientes, but he presented his resignation once again to Congress on 28 February and it was quickly accepted. He was succeeded by Pedro P. Peña, who lasted until 22 March 1912. Every one of the twenty-two days of his ephemeral presidency was marked by violence. On 22 March Peña was succeeded by Emiliano González Navero, who ran into great difficulty with a large loan made to the state by the Portuguese manager of the Asunción–Buenos Aires railway and quit on 15 August. All the time Colonel Jara was plotting his return, but he was wounded in communal fighting in the town of Paraguarí. With his intestines hanging out, he was captured by his enemies and brought back to Asunción, where on 15 May he died in atrocious pain in the company of Gondra, whom he had pitched out of power the previous year. Eduardo Schaerer was voted into power on 15 August and survived a full four-year term. No novelist would have dared to write such an impossible tale: no reader would have believed it.

The Liberals' period in power continued until a short, bloody civil war in 1947; thereafter various Colorado factions governed until the advent of Lugo sixty-one years later.

Meanwhile, in the 1930s Paraguay was to outsiders romantically involved once again in a new and incomprehensible war, Paraguay's barefoot troops beating off equally barefoot Bolivian troops in the waterless desert of the Chaco. David Zook, a US historian of the war, described how much of the Chaco consisted of clumps of thick thorny bush where the sap of spiny cactus had to serve as water and the air was full of millions of bloodsucking insects. In the rainy season the land was transformed into swamps, while in the hot season a fine dust rose up in clouds, penetrating everything. Zook says it was the first war whose outcome was determined by the ability to deliver supplies to the troops. Not for nothing is one of Asunción's main avenues named Choferes del Chaco in honour of the drivers who along dirt tracks and on rickety vehicles took the soldiers what they needed.

Thousands died of thirst on both sides. Battles depended on each side's reserves of transport to provide water and other supplies. Horses were left to starve to death without fodder or water as commanders kept what supplies they could for their troops. In the end gallant Paraguay came out of the Chaco War a little ahead of the Bolivians, who had started hostilities overconfident of their superior equipment and the limited strategic gifts of Hans von Kundt, the German general whom they were employing. They had to sack him in the middle of the fighting.

The genuinely popular hero of the Chaco War, General José Félix Estigarribia, became president. In February 1940 he gave himself full powers and decreed a new authoritarian constitution. But he died in an air accident in September 1940. In the absence of a Council of State or a Chamber of Deputies, which the new constitution had called for but which had not yet been established, senior officers decided that another general, Higinio Morínigo, should take over for sixty days to prepare elections and oversee the installation of an elected president. Morínigo stayed almost eight years.

TWO YEARS: SIX PRESIDENTS

General Morínigo was overthrown in 1948, and for the second time in the twentieth century Paraguayan politicians demonstrated their capacity for self-parody by engendering six heads of state in two years. Morínigo was superseded by Juan Manuel Frutos, who stayed three months. Then came the ultra-nationalist Natalicio González, a journalist and author, for five months – he then went off as ambassador to Mexico and never came back; General Ramón Rolón, a veteran of the Chaco War and later defence minister, was in the palace for twenty-eight days; then came Felipe Molas López for seven months, punctuated by a brief coup. Federico Chaves (leader of the Chavistas and a Colorado) arrived in 1949 and stayed until he was pushed out by his fellow Colorado, Stroessner, in 1954.

3 | STROESSNER POUNCES

The man who was principally responsible for the messy, corrupt chaos of poverty for the many amid luxury for the few that Lugo was to take over in 2008 was a man of courage, overweening ambition and slyness. His actions shaped the way the young Lugo grew up and intimately affected Lugo's family. His principal tool of government was corruption; when that did not work, he used terror.

Alfredo Stroessner Matiauda was born in Asunción on 3 November 1912 to Hugo Wilhelm Stroessner from Hof in Upper Bavaria, who arrived in South America in his twenties, and his wife Heriberta Matiauda. The immigrant ended up in the Argentine city of Posadas but then found prospects better on the Paraguayan side of the River Paraná. There he established a small brewery which did not last very long, so he started teaching mathematics and doing bookkeeping for local businesses. He met Heriberta, the daughter of a small farmer who cultivated a small patch of *mate*, and married her on 24 October 1904. Stroessner and his new bride were never wealthy. Two of their children, Vicente and Hugo, died, but Alfredo junior and his sister Heriberta lived on. His blond-red hair earned him the nickname of 'Rubio', or 'Blondie'. By the river he acquired a taste for fishing which never left him.

His father wanted him to stick at his books, join the army and eventually become a general but, as there was no secondary school in Asunción, he was sent across the Paraná to Posadas in Argentina, where he had cousins, the children of his mother's brothers and sisters. In 1929 the sixteen-year-old Blondie was sent to military school in Asunción, where his taste for mathematics pointed him towards a career in the artillery.

Within three years Paraguay was at war over the Chaco and the nineteen-year-old cadet went off with the 6th Infantry Regiment and was at Boquerón in the Chaco when Paraguayans achieved their first victory over the enemy. He was promoted to second lieutenant in October 1932. Two months later he was transferred to the artillery and given the command of a group of mortars, and fought in a long series of engagements.

According to an official version, at a fort called The Strongest, during one of the Paraguayans' more calamitous encounters with the Bolivians, he barely escaped with his life under heavy fire; another young subaltern threw himself on Stroessner and both rolled into a shell hole and safety. After the war, during which he got his first sniff of military politics from those officers who were planning a better future after the end of hostilities, he went on an artillery course in Brazil, where he got good marks. On the last day of 1945 he reached the rank of lieutenant colonel. He was well placed to enter the world of serious Paraguayan politics.

He was a soldier to the marrow of his bones, who, apart from whisky and Kent or Camel cigarettes, did not favour consuming anything more than plain, home-cooked food. He was keen on fish, especially salmon, and until the end of his time in Paraguay he enjoyed catching them. As he got older he became increasingly taciturn; he baulked at those who tried to advise him. He preferred the company of military men over civilians and was never happier than when he was in an army context. At the presidential residence in Asunción, Mburuvicha Roga, he liked to play cards with his companions and could hold his own in chess matches with experienced players. He enjoyed the company of humbler Paraguayans, to whom he liked to talk in Guaraní.

Though there is some mystery about the date of his wedding, it probably took place in 1949. Stroessner's wife was Eligia. They had three children, the first two, it seems, born before their wedding. They also adopted another. Throughout her married life Eligia had to suffer her husband's continuous unfaithfulness with stoicism. It was the death of a son through alcohol and drugs shortly after the dictator's overthrow which appeared to have affected her most.

Stroessner's constant companion for many years was María Estela Legal, known as Ñata, whom he met when she was fourteen. He took her to many public functions and spent weekends with her at a house near the River Acaray in eastern Paraguay. They had two daughters; the elder, María Estela, was the favourite of all his children. He attended her wedding, dancing with her and her mother. Despite it being an open secret that Ñata was 'the second first lady', she conducted herself with circumspection and had much influence on the dictator, acting as a link between him and prominent businessmen. Good-looking and elegant, she offered him much that his wife, who had no ambition beyond being a housewife, could not.

Yet Stroessner never lost his desire for all varieties of female flesh, and the younger the better. Ñata was the longest-lasting but not by a long way the only fourteen-year-old who took the dictator's fancy. In

1950, when he was thirty-eight, at Paraguarí where he was stationed, he was introduced to another called Tina by one of the White Russian officers who had made new careers in Paraguay. After two years he took her with him to Asunción and had her lodged with one of his relations. She became pregnant and, escaping from her lodgings, took up with other men. Miryam, another mistress, had another of his daughters, who was about seventeen at the time he was overthrown in 1989. There was a twenty-year-old called Blanca Gómez, who had no children by him and went off to the USA after the 1989 coup in which Stroessner was overthrown. Women with whom he had no more than passing affairs, many of whom were eager to have them, were paid off or married to men at Stroessner's court, who were well rewarded for taking them off his hands.

For more rapid relationships the dictator relied on a retired lieutenant colonel, Leopoldo Perrier. Known as Popol, he had got to know Stroessner in the Chaco War, kept a brothel, and made it his business to find young girls around the country whom he could present to his master. For a time Stroessner frequented the premises regularly, often at the beginning of the day, summoning ministers there for consultations. In his chronicle of Stroessner's times Bernardo Neri Farina recounts how his liking for holding parties in barracks with plenty of alcohol and women led him to add to his official titles of 'The First Sportsman of Paraguay' and 'The First Worker of Paraguay' the unofficial title of 'The First Phallus of Paraguay'. One officer who was repelled by the dictator's habits later wrote that he turned 'the Palacio de López [the presidential palace] into a whores' bedroom'. In Stroessner's day bars and brothels multiplied.

THE LUGO FAMILY

Fernando Armindo Lugo Méndez, nicknamed 'Nono', was born the youngest of seven children on 19 May 1951 at San Solano, a farming town in the north of the department of Itapúa in the south-eastern corner of Paraguay, as Stroessner was planning his bid for the presidency. His father, Guillermo Lugo Ramos, worked on the railway and was a figure in the local Colorado party structure, and his wife, Maximina Pérez Fleitas de Méndez, was a teacher – the Spanish convention is for surnames to consist of the father's followed by the mother's. Mercedes, his only sister, became the First Lady of Paraguay after his election, while Domingo Darío, who died at six months in 1945, is buried, in accordance with local practice, as an *angelito* (little angel) a few metres from where the family house used to stand.

The characteristics of Stroessner's long dictatorship were being forged in Lugo's early years – the general's complete dominance of the long-established Colorado party; the ease with which he was able to prolong his tyranny year after year with no political opposition through a mixture of guile and terror; a strong alliance with successive US governments; and an increasing gulf between himself and the Church, which, in the absence of effective civilian opposition, was left as the most important centre of resistance to his rule.

It is difficult to overestimate the effect of the Stroessner dictatorship and the Colorado party on the course of the greater part of Fernando Lugo's life. He was nearly four when Stroessner became president, and was a promising priest approaching thirty-eight and tipped to become a bishop when the dictator was overthrown in 1989. When Stroessner died in exile in August 2006, Lugo had already resigned after more than a decade as a bishop and was on his way to a life in politics. The Colorado party was to rule for another two years until it ceded power to Lugo in August 2008.

San Solano had once been a prosperous little place. It had a sawmill owned by a Uruguayan company which cut down trees in the neighbour-hood, sawed them up and dispatched them by rail to Asunción, from where they were sent downriver to Montevideo or Buenos Aires. At one point the firm had 1,000 ox-drawn carts to move the lumber.

San Solano was also the birthplace in 1917 of Epifanio (Epiphany) Méndez Fleitas, Maximina's brother. Epifanio's shadow fell over everyone who lived there. The Lugos, Guillermo and Maximina, would not have named their fourth child Epifanio had they not been proud of such an important figure of national repute. The highs and lows of the career of the elder Epifanio certainly made the Lugo family aware of the rough practicalities of Paraguayan politics. A poet, writer and composer, as well as politician, he was to play a key role in the rise to supreme power of Stroessner. At the peak of the sawmill's fortunes and of Epifanio's career, San Solano was the first place in the department with drinking water and electric light, and it had an all-weather road to take the timber down to the railway. But after Epifanio fell out with the dictator in 1956 San Solano was allowed to rot as a punishment.

Epifanio was a charismatic member of the Colorado party, which he had joined in 1938. As an active student politician he participated in the efforts to maintain General Higinio Morínigo in power in the wars of 1947, and he served President Felipe Molas, who was in power for much of 1948. He also had a great musical talent, which helped his popularity in politics. He created the Orquesta San Solano, a group named after his birthplace, and was well known as a composer and lyricist. During the presidency of Federico Chaves, who governed from 11 September 1949 until ousted by General Alfredo Stroessner in 1954, Epifanio, the young Lugo's uncle, was given a spell as police chief in the capital and then became president of the Central Bank.

In that post the multi-talented Epifanio was seen by his often paranoid political opponents as too much in love with the power of the state – perhaps even tempted to flirt with communism. He was also too close to Perón in Argentina, whose visit to Chaves in Asunción in October 1953 Epifanio had prepared by pushing the idea of a customs union between Argentina and Paraguay. Worse, Epifanio was seen as not sufficiently understanding of the interests of the powerful ranching lobby. Towards the end of 1953 influential army officers pressed Chaves to dismiss him since he was standing in the way of the doubling of the price of beef that the cattle raisers wanted, claiming, not without reason, that he might be plotting to seize the presidency for himself. Chaves sacked him from the bank on 6 January 1954. Epifanio went on to ally himself with the promising Stroessner. He did not have long to wait until Stroessner acceded to supreme power.

Epifanio had been in the bad books of the US embassy. In a dispatch dated 4 January 1956 urging the State Department to mobilize the International Monetary Fund to assist Stroessner, the ambassador, Arthur Ageton, a retired admiral, recalled the uncomfortable three years that the USA had undergone when Epifanio was at the height of his powers. The envoy said that he had dominated the politics of the bank, discouraged the development of industry and agriculture, wasted the monetary reserves of the country and adopted an unfriendly attitude towards Washington.

As the weeks passed, divisions within the Colorados and the military deepened, with the cavalry and the police lining up behind the president and the rest pushing for his overthrow. On the morning of 3 May 1954 the commander of the cavalry decreed the arrest of a cavalry major who was a political ally of Stroessner and Méndez. In an act of serious insubordination Stroessner verbally attacked President Chaves for allowing the action, and later an infantry battalion physically attacked the police seen to be backing Chaves. As the sound of firing drowned the sound of the Philharmonic Orchestra performing in Asunción's Municipal Theatre, Chaves fled to the military college. Its commander, sadly for the president, was in the Stroessner camp. The two were talking when a captain broke in and announced to Chaves, 'Your Excellency, you are under arrest.' Another tragicomic Latin American military coup had been sprung. Chaves was out, Stroessner was master of Paraguay, and the futility of the country's supposed democracy was again made patent.

Stroessner, who had plotted against five presidents, was declared 'constitutional president' on 15 August 1954 to serve out Chaves's uncompleted term of office

When Stroessner took power he put Epifanio back in his job in the bank with the financial patronage which that bestowed. The Lugo family thereby acquired that most useful attribute, a member of the family with access to the president. But such was the dictator's paranoia about a man who was a civilian but had a following in the army, and who made no secret of his desire to take over as president at the end of the newly installed Stroessner's term, that Epifanio was unlikely to keep his job for long. On 22 December 1955 Stroessner sacked him from the Central Bank, and by January 1956 he had been sent on a mission abroad for Stroessner from which he was never allowed to return. The Lugos had their moment of influence, but it was a brief one.

The personal tastes – and fears – of the new head of state were well captured in a report from the US embassy on 1 June 1955 of a party on a ranch in the Chaco the previous week, which Stroessner attended and where he had decided the guests were to be mostly army captains and majors. He did not want senior officers or civilian politicians present, despite the fact that local Colorado notables had been keen to attend. Stroessner and a party arrived by plane and on arrival took out their pistols and started shooting at any target that presented itself – birds, telegraph poles, tin cans or bottles – and the dictator demonstrated he was a good shot. He had with him an assistant whose job was to check his food for poison, and when the host started to prepare a whisky for his guest he was told to put the bottle unopened on the president's table. After the *asado* (barbecue), he and an officer settled down to a long game of chess, liberally lubricated with alcohol. When that was over he settled down for an hour of two of swapping blue jokes before flying back to Asunción.

Officers of the sort who were at the *asado* had reason to be merry. Captain Andrés Rodríguez, whose daughter Martha was to marry Stroessner's son Hugo Alfredo, had a good nose for politics. After Stroessner's successful putsch of 1955, Rodríguez, then a captain, was delighted with the situation. As he made his way to the office of the commander of the cavalry, he exclaimed in Guaraní with considerable foresight, '*Ko'ápe ñamanda aréta, ha ñande ricopáta*' (We're going to govern for a long time and we'll all be very rich'). And so it was to be.

4 Lugo with a cousin in the village of Hohenau.

As Fernando Lugo was growing up quietly enough in Encarnación the new dictator was entering on a long and friendly relationship with successive US presidents in Washington. He also started a long-drawn-out succession of hostilities with the Catholic Church in Asunción.

Stroessner got off to a good start in his courtship of the USA. In September 1954, shortly after his formal installation in the presidency, Washington appointed Ageton, with whom the Paraguayan, always partial to other officers in the armed forces, soon formed a close relationship. The admiral encouraged him to put into force the Law for the Defence of Democracy, Law 294, which reached the highest peak of the oxymoronic in politics. It forbade any expression of protest against the government and proscribed Marxism, making any formulation of it illegal and turning any formulators into criminals. Open or secret members of the small Paraguayan Communist Party were *ipso facto* committing an offence. The law decreed that any public servant who by commission or omission failed to denounce anyone committing acts contrary to its spirit and letter should be immediately dismissed. It was the cornerstone of several generations of *pyragüés* (spies), whose word could involve any Paraguayan and bring them the often bestially cruel attentions of the police.

On 23 June 1956 Eisenhower, US president between 1953 and 1961, together with his brother Milton and his ultra-conservative Secretary of State John Foster Dulles, received Stroessner at the US ambassador's residence in Panama City. Panama was at the time a client state of Washington's which had ensured its independence from Colombia in 1903 and which maintained the Canal Zone, a strip through the centre of the country which contained the transoceanic canal, and which was returned to Panama in 1979. According to a State Department account of the meeting, Stroessner said he hoped there would not be a Third World War but, if there were, Paraguay would play its role in any part of the world, contributing its men and its spirit. Paraguay, Stroessner told the US president, was 100 per cent anti-communist and would continue to be so.

Eisenhower agreed to aid Paraguay in a number of projects it was seeking to promote, since the dictator had also bid for the sort of level of financial aid Bolivia was getting from the USA following the revolution of 1952. Such aid had not been given to Paraguay, with whom Bolivia had fought the Chaco War. Before long cash was flowing out of the treasuries of the US Export-Import Bank and the international financial organizations, and between 1954 and 1960 Paraguay received the (for then) enormous amount of US$60 million.

Bernardo Neri, Stroessner's biographer, says in his book *El Último Supremo* that the start of the flow of foreign aid funds to Paraguay was the start of the dictator's policy of buying the support of his opponents. It was the beginning of the country's unchallenged reputation in South America for corruption against which Lugo inveighed as a churchman and a politician. In monetary terms Paraguay's corruption and financial trickery under Stroessner never amounted to very much on the world scale. Yet corruption thoroughly polluted Paraguayan society and, as he frequently declared, made Lugo ashamed.

The US president was responsible for a more sinister gift to Paraguay, as was revealed in 1992 when Martín Almada, a leading Paraguayan human rights worker, unearthed the 5 tons of hitherto secret government and police documents now labelled the 'Archive of Terror'. Eisenhower sent Colonel Robert Thierry of the US army to Paraguay from May 1956 to March 1958 to teach torture techniques to the Dirección Nacional de Asuntos Técnicos, the National Department for Technical Affairs, better known as '*la Técnica*', which started operating as a torture centre in 1956 inside the police headquarters in Asunción. There thousands of the dictator's victims were subjected to the most inhuman treatment that the USA and Paraguay could invent. In the records of Washington's foreign aid organization, the Thierry mission was euphemistically referred to as 'training in public administration', and it started yielding its bitter fruits as Lugo grew into boyhood.

Thierry was one of a number of such officers with US police experience who were stationed in Latin America at this time, with the job of making governments of the region that were friendly to Washington more familiar with modern methods of torture and bolstering the concept of the 'national security state'. The record of these governments – notably Brazil, Uruguay, Chile, El Salvador and Guatemala – shows that they were generally successful in their mission. They used simulated drownings, immersion in baths full of faeces, recordings of the screams of relatives themselves undergoing torture and the panoply of other methods that were to be practised by the French, the Israelis and the US troops themselves in Iraq.

One of the best-known members of this team, which ranged over Latin America, was Dan Mitrione, who was active in Brazil after the US-assisted military coup of 1964. The techniques he sought to perfect and impart included electric shocks to the genitals, electrified needles inserted under the nails and slow strangulation. The motto he insisted his pupils learn was 'the right pain at the right moment in the right amount for the desired effect'.

An interview with him quoted in the *New York Times* in 1979 had him saying:

> It is very important to know beforehand whether we have the luxury of letting the subject die ...
>
> Before all else, you must be efficient. You must cause only the damage that is strictly necessary, not a bit more. We must control our tempers in any case. You have to act with the efficiency and cleanliness of a surgeon and with the perfection of an artist ...

According to an account by John Stockwell, author of *In Search of Enemies* and a former member of the US Central Intelligence Agency familiar with Mitrione's work, he had beggars seized from the streets and turned them into guinea pigs on whom his pupils could practise their new-found skills. When the beggars lost consciousness they were revived with the injection of vitamins, after which their agonies resumed.

From Brazil Mitrione was sent on to Uruguay in 1969, where he was assigned to the office of the US Agency for International Development in Montevideo to help the fight against the Tupamaro guerrillas. After years in South America he was becoming well known to his victims and he was seized by the Tupamaros, who demanded the release of 150 of their people from prison. The Uruguayan government rejected their demand and, sadly for him, Mitrione's lifeless body was later found on the rear seat of a stolen car.

For the USA in 1956 Stroessner's Paraguay had two advantages: it was not bellicose towards other countries, as were Britain and France, which that year formed a secret alliance with Israel to invade Egypt and take its canal back from President Nasser, who had nationalized it; nor was it sympathetic to the USSR, which mobilized its troops in order to snuff out the Hungarian government, which was seeking autonomy from Moscow.

VATICAN II: A REVOLUTION IN THE CHURCH

As Stroessner was being caught up in a mutually profitable relationship with Washington the Paraguayan Church was caught up in an unstoppable process of modernization or, to use the Vatican's Italian term, *aggiornamento*, which had been inaugurated a few years earlier. Though Lugo was only three when the process got under way, its effects were worldwide and were to influence him greatly.

On 28 October 1958, at the age of seventy-six, the charismatic and humbly born Angelo Roncalli was elected pope, taking the name John XXIII. He was a world away from his aloof, princely predecessor Eugenio Pacelli, Pius XII. Roncalli's parents had been sharecroppers, working a 5-hectare plot. Half the mulberry leaves they grew to feed silkworms, half their rough wine and half their milk and veal went to the landlords. They fed their thirteen children and other family members with the other half.

All his life Roncalli tried to remain approachable and, accurately or not, a number of jokes were told of him. One involved the stationmaster who worked near Sotto il Monte, the village where Roncalli was born and who asked the pontiff during one of the latter's visits home, '*Santità*, how many people work in the Vatican?' 'Oh, about half, I think,' the pope was supposed to have replied.

Conscious that he was in the autumn of his days, John XXIII adopted ambitious initiatives on his election which astonished the many who had regarded him as an old man unlikely to be an innovator. But he came to be known as the man who 'flung open the windows of the Vatican'. He certainly turned his back on extreme pronouncements such as those embodied in the Catechism of San Alberto or those made a century before by Pius IX, who railed against freedom of religion, of conscience and of worship, and in the last words of his Syllabus of Errors of 1864 declared, 'the pontiff neither can nor ought to be reconciled with progress, liberalism and modern civilization'. In 1870 he presided over the First Vatican Council as it proclaimed that a pope was infallible on those occasions when he addressed the whole Church on matters of faith or morals.

To the extreme distress of many conservatives there were, under John XXIII, the beginnings of a rapprochement with Nikita Khrushchev's Soviet Union, with which many in the Vatican and in the West had been at daggers drawn throughout the cold war. On the occasion of the Conference of Non-Aligned Nations in Belgrade in September 1961, the pope sent a friendly, encouraging message to a gathering advocating nuclear disarmament and which, for that and many other reasons, European and US cold warriors despised. John's gesture received an immediate response from Moscow. In an interview published in *Pravda* on 21 September 1961 the Russian leader commented:

> John XXIII pays tribute to reason. From all parts of the world there rises up a desire for peace that we can only approve of ... It is not that we fear God's judgement, in which as an atheist I do not believe, but we welcome the appeal to negotiate no matter where it comes from. Will ardent Catholics like John F. Kennedy, Konrad Adenauer and others heed the Pope's warning?

This was followed on 25 November by a congratulatory telegram from the Soviet leader on John's eightieth birthday. According to Peter Hebblethwaite's masterly biography, the pontiff commented, 'Well, it's better than a slap in the face.' He later said in a more serious mood, 'There is something going on in the world ... Today we have received a sign from Providence.' The reply to Khrushchev rapidly came back from Rome: 'His Holiness Pope John XXIII thanks you for your good wishes and for his part sends to the whole Russian people cordial wishes for the increase and strengthening of universal peace by means of understanding based on human brotherhood: to this end he prays fervently.'

In such an atmosphere – and after a blizzard of preparation and overcoming sabotage, ambushes and pitfalls contrived by the conservatives – the solemn inauguration of the Second Vatican Council brought the bishops from all over the world to St Peter's in Rome in October 1962. Despite the fact that the eleven-year-old may not have been able to follow the politics that swirled around it, the Council, which was attended by bishops he either knew personally or whose attitude he was aware of, was followed by the pious young Lugo. To the intense anger of the far right, including many in Rome who stood four-square behind the ideas of Pius IX, Vatican II sought a return to the simplicity of the gospels, started refashioning a church of the poor and made a bonfire of antiquated practices, much in accordance with the spirit of those such as Las Casas. On his deathbed in May 1963, with Vatican II in full flood, John XXIII gave a final message: 'Today more than ever we are called to serve mankind as such, and not merely Catholics; to defend above all and everywhere the rights of the human person and not merely those of the Catholic Church.'

The churchmen of Paraguay played their own not negligible part in putting into practice the resolutions of Vatican II, and this did not bode well for the Church's relationship with the dictatorship.

Stroessner's cosy relationship with successive US governments meant that each depended on the other during the long years of the cold war. They were brought together, it was often said, in the cause of anti-communism. The reality was subtly different from appearances. The Paraguayan and the US sides looked at each other less in ideological terms and more in terms of the help each could give the other in retaining power.

For years Washington used the supposed threat of communism, which was never a great force in the region, as a screen. Behind such a screen it could pursue its own political and business interests and at the same time keep at bay the prying eyes of Europe and other nations outside the western hemisphere, as well as those of the United Nations. Washington preferred to see international matters decided at the Organization of American States, a US-run body in Washington, rather than at the UN, where the USSR had a powerful voice and the possibility of halting actions it did not like through the veto it enjoyed as a permanent member of the Security Council.

In the 1950s the case of Father Ramón Talavera, the priest in charge of the Virgen del Carmen parish in the capital, blew up, signalling the first public encounter between Church and dictatorship. The priest was from a comfortable middle-class family with good Colorado credentials, but he was not ready to countenance Stroessner's violence. He had been active in the Young Catholic Workers movement, in which Ramón Bogarín, soon to become a bishop, had been a leading light. The parish priest was outraged when the newly installed dictator ordered the closure of its radio broadcasts and its magazine, both of which Talavera edited.

At the end of 1957 things got worse. Talavera delivered a strong verbal attack on the military after they had planned the expulsion of the inhabitants of a slum that occupied ground near the barracks of the Presidential Escort Battalion. Army officers wanted it to build houses for themselves. On 22 February 1958, with Catholic Action and the Liberal

Party, he called a meeting in front of the National Pantheon in the capital's main square, which brought out 2,000 people. He announced that Paraguayans should stand up 'to save the country' because 'the hour of Paraguayan dignity has arrived'. He demanded a general amnesty and freedom of speech and criticized the size of military budgets at a moment when country people were starving. People, he said, had to 'stand up against tyranny'. The police went into action with great brutality and Stroessner went on to demand that priests favourable to him should come out against Talavera and praise the dictator's bountiful policies. That did not happen, but Juan José Aníbal Mena Porta, the conservative archbishop of Asunción, given the priest's undeniable popularity, went back on years of silence and brought out a pastoral letter criticizing the government and asking for more political freedom. He also told Talavera to stop making public pronouncements. On 1 August 1958, a fortnight before the dictator was due to celebrate a renewal of his grip on power, Talavera went on hunger strike.

He chose his moment well as the dictator was due to start another term a fortnight later. On 27 August Talavera backed a workers' strike and was with them when they took refuge in the church of Maria Auxilidora, where the police attacked them. In this he was backed by Ismael Rolón, the priest in charge of the parish, who was later to become archbishop of Asunción.

A furious Stroessner expelled Talavera to Argentina on 8 November, the first of a long list of distinguished Catholics to be exiled by the dictator. He got back to Paraguay in August 1959 but was again exiled. The priest took refuge in Buenos Aires, where he founded an anti-Stroessner organization called Christian Crusade, which called for the dictator's overthrow in every communications medium it could reach.

Stroessner's fight with Talavera coincided with worries in Washington and Asunción about the success of the Cuban revolution in the first days of 1959. Encouraged by the news from Havana, the left tried to launch a series of guerrilla campaigns over the next few years with names harking back to the War of the Triple Alliance, such as Columna Mariscal López and Columna Ytororó, but they were soon mopped up with US help.

By that time the Church was taking an increasingly combative attitude towards the dictatorship. For instance, Josu Arketa, a Spanish Franciscan friar, was expelled from Paraguay in 1962 for his uncompromising opposition to Stroessner on Radio Caritas, a Church radio.

The Church's new combative attitude was bolstered by the foundation in 1960 of the Catholic University in Asunción, which helped to spread the new thinking of Vatican II in the country. That work was backed up by a new periodical, *Comunidad*, which the bishops strongly supported from 1963. The results were soon visible. In 1963 the usually cautious episcopal conference produced a pastoral letter, *El problema social Paraguayo* (The social problem of Paraguay), which was as strong as it was unexpected. It demanded real agrarian reform that would end the intense concentration of land ownership in few hands amid the extreme poverty of the majority. The letter was put together under the influence of three figures who had had direct experience of the new Vatican Council and who were all to become bishops – Ismael Rolón, whom we have seen collaborating with Talavera, Aníbal Marichevich and Ramón Bogarín, who during his time as a parish priest in the capital had been influential in founding the Young Catholic Workers in 1941, when his uncle, Juan Sinforiano Bogarín, was archbishop of Asunción.

Rolón made few concessions to the dictator. When he was made bishop of Caacupé, a popular pilgrimage centre, he called off an annual procession in protest against Stroessner's violent clampdown on peasants who were trying to organize themselves. After he was named archbishop of Asunción he resigned from Stroessner's Council of State, protested against the imprisonment of innocent people and inveighed against the forcible closure of *ABC Color* and Radio Ñandutí.

The close nature of the relationships among the small group who headed the Church in the small society that is Paraguay was typified when, shortly after his presidential inauguration, Lugo visited the home of the retired ninety-four-year-old Ismael Rolón in a suburb of the capital to give him a replica of the presidential sash as a mark of honour.

Action for reform was not confined to pastoral letters. The bishops also threw their weight behind the Ligas Agrarias Campesinas, the Peasant Agrarian Leagues, which demanded change and an end to the woeful concentration of land in the hands of a few.

When Fernando Lugo was five months old the family went off to Encarnación, the capital of the department of Itapúa beside the Paraná river, where the young Fernando was to spend his early years. Few places in Paraguay needed reform more than his new home. His father Guillermo was to make a living as a railwayman with a job at the station at Encarnación. The youngsters grew up in modest circumstances. As a young child Lugo was keen on playing marbles. Later he and his siblings played football in the street, though he did well at basketball as well. For pocket money he sometimes sold coffee and sandwiches in the street. He had a bicycle and acquired a love of motorcycles which later blossomed. (He was keen to confess his weakness for motorcycles

5 Lugo with friends, Encarnación.

at the time of his election and assumption of office, being photographed widely in the saddle.)

But the city that became Fernando Lugo's home had a baleful background. Until well into the twentieth century what prosperity it enjoyed stemmed from two interlocking trades both dominated by '*turcos*' or traders from the Levant, those of timber and *yerba mate*, alongside what was to all intents and purposes slavery. The slaves were there to fell the trees and work on the plantations.

The traders ran sidelines in prostitution, known as the white slave trade, and the smuggling of goods across the river between Paraguay and the Argentine city of Posadas opposite it. Girls and women were bought and sold with the same aplomb as the agricultural products and contraband. The labourers were called *mensú*, monthly paid workers. Recruited from country districts, they arrived in Encarnación barefoot, hungry and in rags. There they were given a bed, an advance on their pay and somewhere to sleep. Booze and women were provided and the next day they were packed in river craft and sent off to Argentina or wherever there was work. As has been the case with people-trafficking in Europe, their advance was swallowed up by the bills the labour agents charged them for the 'services' they had received, and they went off with virtually no chance of paying off their 'debts'. They had little alternative to living in servitude. The trade was well known but neither Liberals nor Colorados, Paraguay's traditional political parties founded in the late nineteenth century, felt moved to interfere in it.

In the days of Fernando's youth Paraguay, with hardly one and a half million inhabitants, was at the bottom of the pile of South American states, and its infrastructure reflected this. The journey between Encarnación and the capital obliged the traveller to take his life in his hands; there was no bridge over the River Tebicuary at Villa Florida, so until 1968, when Lugo was a teenager, travellers had to trust themselves and their vehicles to a rickety raft. Such was the principal road link between the centre of the country and the outside world. Only the smallest fraction of the road system was paved, and what street lighting there was consisted of candles in lamps.

Not one of Paraguay's cities boasted piped water. Running water there certainly was. It ran down the streets of Asunción and other centres when it rained since they had no drainage system. Because of the lack of such a system the air was constantly full of the smell of faeces. Along the capital's streets would clang ancient second-hand tramcars bought and imported from Brussels, which still bore the admonition 'Do not spit' in French and Dutch, the two official languages of the Belgian capital.

The young Lugo was no more than eight years old when the first twitch of guerrilla activity in Paraguay came in 1959, the year Fidel Castro came to power in Cuba. It was soon eliminated. In December of that year a group of eighty guerrillas did cross the northern frontier from Brazil, but no evidence emerged that the recently installed government in Havana had anything to do with the action, apart perhaps from setting an example that the Paraguayans wanted to follow. The majority were picked up within a week, with a few escaping to Argentina.

Encarnación had for long been one of Paraguay's main points of contact with the world – during the presidency of Francia it was almost the only one. Some thought it was Paraguayan territory, some thought it was part of Argentina, no one knowing for sure. For decades, though with increasing irregularity, a train puffed the 1,000 kilometres across the pampas from Buenos Aires, bringing passengers for Paraguay. They and their coaches would be put on the train ferry and taken across the River Paraná to complete the exhausting journey to Asunción. The rail service all but disappeared, but the city continued to be the source of goods, legal or smuggled, between the two countries. It was not until 1989, just after Stroessner's overthrow, that a road bridge more than two kilometres long allowing vehicles to drive across the Paraná was opened by the newly installed President Rodríguez and his Argentine counterpart, Carlos Menem, both rich men fully conversant with the political and financial practices in their countries.

Otherwise plunged in the deepest mediocrity, Encarnación did, however, have one outstanding feature near by – the ruins of Trinidad.

If the young Lugo had not been conscious of the dictatorship in his early childhood, he became conscious of it during his school years: the actions and omissions of Stroessner were to shape the young man's life directly until the dictator's death in 1999, and indirectly through the continuing social blight that continued to affect Paraguay thereafter. The thoughts and actions of Lugo are not easily comprehensible outside the context of what Paraguayans call '*stronismo*', the ways of Stroessner and the Colorado party he dominated.

Both the future bishop's parents were punished under Stroessner because of Epifanio's actions and, like Epifanio, three of Fernando's brothers went into exile. His father, Guillermo, for instance, who had been a leading *epifanista*, was arrested on 28 December 1962 after a denunciation of him made at work. He was taken to the police head-quarters in Asunción, a noted torture centre, when Fernando was eleven. There Guillermo was joined by more than a score of other Colorado leaders suspected by the dictator of disloyalty to him. The tortures he

6 Lugo (fifth from right) with friends during military service.

7 Lugo receives school-leaving certificate from Alfredo Stroessner, 1969.

suffered there, including the treatment that has become notorious in the USA as 'waterboarding', did serious damage to his kidneys, which was later to cause his death. After three of his brothers had been tortured at the hands of Stroessner's police, as Lugo was later to recall in an interview with BBC Radio in February 2009, there was much pressure in the family for him to forget any ideas of going into politics.

When doing his part-time military service, for instance, in his late teens in Encarnación, Fernando Lugo had his own first personal experience of *stronismo*. Like the rest of young Paraguayan males, Lugo was obliged to do such military service, which was completed during school holidays in a unit called Cimefor, the Centre for Military Training for Students and the Formation of Reserve Officers. Here Lugo excelled, and his keenness put him on the way to being declared the best young recruit in the country of his intake in 1969. But senior officers noted who he was and decided that it would not be fitting if someone bearing the name of Méndez should be singled out for distinction in a military ceremony in Asunción which was likely to be presided over by Stroessner. *ABC Color* recounts[1] how the marking was doctored and the distinction went to another boy.

Between 1968 and 1973, as he grew into manhood, he continued to

---

1. *ABC Color*, 15 August 2008.

be seen as clever and attractive, but his teachers and friends saw as well that there was a wilder side to him. He sported a Beatles haircut and appreciated their music as well as that of other groups. He took time off from his serious reading to devote to comics.

Disappointed in his inability to pursue a military career, and warned off politics, he gained a teaching certificate in 1969. It was given to him in a ceremony by Stroessner himself, as a photograph that surfaced during the election campaign shows. Lugo, dressed in an immaculate white shirt, is seen shaking hands with the dictator, dressed in a dark suit with a tie and a handkerchief peeping out of his breast pocket. Each of them shows the most wan of smiles, much as if sizing up the other for the political contests upon which they would soon be embarking. Lugo went on briefly to teach in a state school, but in March 1970 he finally decided on the religious life and entered the Paraguayan novitiate of the Divine Word Missionaries.

4 | VERBISTAS AND LIBERACIONISTAS

As he grew up in Encarnación, Fernando Lugo had had every opportunity of seeing the Divine Word Missionaries and observing their style of life, and the example of many of the members of the order was to be a continuing inspiration to him. Lugo as a bishop and a politician cannot be fully understood without examining the organization to which he committed himself as a young man.

The members of a body formally known as 'the Society of the Divine Word at the Service of the King and Queen of Angels', the Societas Verbi Divini (SVD), known in Italian as '*Verbiti*' and in Spanish as '*Verbistas*', are generally worthy people, but they do not belong to one of the Catholic Church's most renowned and distinguished orders. They have neither the ancient history of the Benedictine monks in their monasteries, who trace their order back to St Benedict of Nursia, who was born around AD 480, nor that order's millennium of architectural monuments from Monte Cassino to Westminster Abbey. (The *Verbistas* therefore avoid the point made by some mischievous English religious critics of the Benedictines, who suggest that the initials of the English Benedictine Congregation can also stand for the phrase 'every bodily comfort'.) Nor do the *Verbistas* have the mystique of the mendicant orders of friars, originally begging for their bread outside their humble friaries, who came into being in the thirteenth century, or the intellectual brilliance of the Dominican friars, in whose ranks Thomas Aquinas set out the foundations of Western theology in the second millennium.

They lack the aura of the Franciscan friars, the followers of Francis of Assisi, the layman from Umbria who celebrated God's creation and whose prayers are increasingly used in a world sensitive to ecological matters. (It was the Franciscans who started early missionary work in America. Indeed, they were the first to found settlements for indigenes in Paraguay.)

Similarly, the *Verbistas* cannot claim the sheer intellectual and political elan of the Jesuits, which they have enjoyed since the days of their foundation by Íñigo de Loyola and Francisco Xavier, the Basques who received papal permission to set up their order in 1540. Since the mid-sixteenth century the Jesuits have provided the papacy with priceless and disciplined spiritual force. Had it not been for the lobbying of the Franciscans in Rome, who objected to Jesuit forms of evangelization in seventeenth-century China and disrupted their efforts, the Society might have converted the Chinese emperor – and doubtless tens of millions of his subjects – to Christianity.

In a revealing interview with the Spanish newspaper *El Periódico* in late 2008, the Jesuit general of the day, Father Adolfo Nicolás Pachón, confessed that there was a basis for the often-held view that members of his order were arrogant: 'This is a weakness we have and it is quite common. This comes from the fact that in the Society we have always insisted on the concern for quality and in-depth formation. The problem is that we are human beings, and we don't realize that that capability has been given to us, it's not because of our pretty face.'

The Society of the Holy Word to which Lugo was to commit himself was founded by Arnold Janssens, the second of ten children, who became a priest in his diocese of Münster in northern Germany in 1861 and initially settled down to the life of a secondary school teacher. At the time, the Catholic Church was in the first stages of the *Kulturkampf* (or struggle of cultures) with Bismarck, the German Chancellor, who, having achieved the establishment of Germany as an empire with Wilhelm, king of Prussia, as its first emperor, was determined to control public education. In order to do that he exiled and sometimes imprisoned Church leaders. Finding bishops and clergy being exiled and sometimes jailed, Janssens had the idea in 1875 of gathering together some of Bismarck's victims who could no longer continue in Germany in a specifically missionary body dedicated to spreading the Catholic faith in other countries. He prudently based his group in a little village of Steijl or Steyl on the River Meuse on the Dutch side of the frontier with Germany. The mission process started four years later, when two members were sent to China.

In 2008 the *Verbistas*, run from their headquarters in the Via dei Verbiti in Rome, totalled 3,900 priests – including some fifty bishops and archbishops – and 6,000 religious brothers working in nearly four hundred parishes throughout the world. With a *soupçon* of ecclesiastical bravado they posted on their website that year, 'The Society of the Divine Word is the only major congregation of religious men which has shown steady growth over the last 30 years.' They took pride in the variety of places where they served.

Chacko Thottumarickal, to take one instance, was in 2002 named first bishop of the newly created diocese of Jhabua. The town lay in a poor region of tribal people not far from Bhopal in India, scene of the 1984 Union Carbide disaster, which killed thousands and left many more blind. Fewer than one person in a hundred in Jhabua – 31,000 out of a total population of 4 million – is a Catholic. The historical connections and the ambition of the order were illustrated by their presence on the northern coast of Papua New Guinea. Much of the island was in the late nineteenth century taken by Germany as a colony. The Society maintained its strong presence for nearly a century after the expulsion of the Germans during the First World War. All but one of the bishops of Madang in the twentieth century were *Verbistas* and the SVD founded the Divine Word University in the 1950s.[2]

At a time when many women were finding vocations in the Church, two orders of nuns were associated with the SVD. (In recent years, before the withering of the numbers of priests and nuns, the irreverent in Rome, of whom there are many, often used to suggest that although God knows everything two facts do escape Him. The first is the exact number of congregations of nuns that exist. The second is how much the Dominicans, the intellectual order of the Church par excellence, think they know.) The popular image of a *Verbista* was of a dedicated person open to being sent by his superiors anywhere in the world, but unlikely to have outstanding intellectual gifts. In 2003 Janssens and Joseph Freinademetz, one of the original missionaries to China, were canonized, after the usual campaign of pious but inexorable lobbying that accompanies these events. No *Verbista*, it seems, had at the time of writing ever been made a cardinal.

By the time Lugo was born the SVD had become well established in Latin America. The first *Verbistas* arrived in Paraguay before the end of the nineteenth century, not long after the foundation of their order. They were attracted by the appeal of Bishop Sinforiano Bogarín, who was to spend half a century as bishop or archbishop in Asunción, and who put them to work in the region of Alto Paraná. They stayed there over the decades and witnessed the transformation of their territory by the massive works built along the Paraná river. They went on to provide the first two bishops, the first a Pole, the second a German, when this chunk of unprepossessing wilderness was carved out and made into a territorial prelature, a sort of second-class diocese which, when it was set up in 1968, clearly had no hope of finding the money to support itself.

By the end of the twentieth century the order was working in Argentina, Bolivia, Brazil, Chile, Colombia, Cuba, Ecuador, Mexico, Nicaragua,

---

2. *Annuario Pontificio* and www.svdcuria.org.

Panama and Uruguay. Its members' views reflected all colours of the spectrum of Church thought.

As Lugo grew up, the best-known *Verbista* in the western hemisphere was undoubtedly Geraldo de Proença Sigaud. He was a champion of extreme right-wing views who was a constant reminder of the deep differences between those who kept to traditional views and those who wanted more openness in the Church. He was appointed archbishop of the remote and beautiful town of Diamantina in the Brazilian state of Minas Gerais in 1960. It had been at the centre of the avalanche of gems and precious metals that flowed from the mines of the region to the Portuguese crown in Lisbon to which the Brazilians owed allegiance.

As a man of the extreme right he was one of the founders in 1960 of a Brazilian association called Family, Tradition and Property (TFP), which aligned itself with the country's most reactionary politicians, including the military officers who overthrew the civilian government of President João Goulart in 1964 with the quiet assistance of the US, British and other Western governments. Sigaud was a particularly bitter adversary of Helder Câmara, archbishop of Olinda and Recife, himself a strong supporter of the liberation theologians. Unsurprisingly perhaps, given that Diamantina's original wealth had been won by the sweat of slaves, Sigaud became an intellectual bulwark of the Brazilian landowners. He wrote and campaigned constantly against the idea of land reform, which would alter the suffocating concentration of income in the hands of the estate owners and upset a social system that had a majority of country people living hungry and illiterate in circumstances of effective slavery.

To the applause of many in the military dictatorship, and in headlong contradiction to the attitude Lugo was later to adopt, Sigaud argued that it was immoral for a Catholic to benefit from the confiscation of another's land, which, he said, went against the seventh and tenth commandments. He drafted a letter to Paul VI which condemned 'communist subversion at times hidden beneath clerical garb', which was signed by a thousand members of the Brazilian social elite, including the wife of the military dictator of the day.

Sigaud was a close associate of Bishop Antônio Castro Meyer, who was excommunicated by Rome in 1988 for his support of Marcel Lefebvre's schismatic movement. Had he himself not resigned from his diocese in 1980 Sigaud might well have ultimately been ejected from the Church in company with Castro Meyer.

The TFP supported strategies of terror and torture against the left and the centre not just in Brazil but in other parts of the region. A book published in Montevideo by TFP in the 1960s, *Izquierdismo en la Iglesia:*

compañero de ruta del comunismo en la larga aventura de los fracasos y las metamorfósis ('The Left in the Church: fellow traveller of communism on the long adventure of failures and metamorphoses') bitterly condemned Carlos Partelli, archbishop of the Uruguayan capital, for 'inflating the show put on by the communists in Uruguay'. Quoting from the bishops' statements, it said, 'almost all the bishops, and a impressive part of the clergy, abandoned the Christian people as they were under attack and favoured the cause which they were obliged to fight'.

The churchmen of Paraguay played their own not negligible part in Vatican II, as did the *Verbistas* of South America. The *Verbista* bishop of La Rioja in the foothills of the Argentina Andes was to give his life for the spirit of Vatican II. In La Rioja, a poor area in the shadow of the Andes to which he was appointed in 1968, Enrique Angelelli had encouraged the very land reform that Sigaud had been railing about and supported the creation of unions of miners, rural workers and domestic workers, as well as cooperatives to make handicrafts, bricks, clocks and bread. Within his diocese was the town of Anillaco, the birthplace and political headquarters of Carlos Menem, who was later to win the Argentine presidency.

In 1973 a group of traders and landowners organized a mob to throw stones at him in Anillaco, disrupt the mass he was trying to celebrate and chase him out of town. For his part the all-too-crafty Menem, always closer to business than to the working people he claimed to represent, withdrew his support for the cooperative on the basis of 'social unrest'. From then on Angelelli, who blamed the TFP for the event in Anillaco, knew he was a marked man. He was to survive only three more years.

Angelelli had been a constant supporter of Vatican II and embraced the ideas of liberation theology, identifying in particular with Argentina's Movement of Priests of the Third World, MSTM, whose inspiration came from the Council. It sought to revolutionize the Church by bringing it closer to the people and throwing out old ideas of discipline, which seemed to be choking the message of the gospel. In Latin America the effect of Vatican II was amplified when the region's bishops met in the Colombian city of Medellín in August 1968 and linked the poverty of a majority of Latin Americans to capitalist practices, which they had no hestitation in condemning. In their final message the bishops turned their back on the sort of conduct that Sigaud and many others had for all too long been happy to adopt and declared they were unable to 'remain indifferent in the face of the tremendous injustices existent in Latin America which keep the majority of our peoples in dismal poverty'.

Preparation for the launching of the first MSTM encounter in May

1968 had gone ahead with the tacit approval of a handful of Argentine bishops, including Angelelli. It was inevitable that there would be a collision between the new movement, which during its ten years of life was to bring together more than five hundred priests, and the military, which, under the leadership of General Juan Carlos Onganía, a Catholic of extreme conservative views, had seized power from the decent elected civilian government of Arturo Illia in 1966. Onganía went about energetically abolishing constitutional guarantees, supporting big business, outlawing strikes, ordering women to wear longer skirts and checking citizens in their homes to make sure they were not committing adultery. He was soon overthrown in a welter of inconsequential governments, military and civilian. Even the aged caudillo Juan Domingo Perón had a new spell in power from October 1973 till his death in July 1974. He was succeeded by his third wife, a former nightclub dancer known as Isabelita.

As Onganía and his military successors had stepped up political repression many of the younger generation of clerics found their voice in the MSTM. In December 1969, more than twenty members of the MSTM went to the presidential palace in Buenos Aires to ask Onganía to do more for Argentine slum dwellers. MSTM statements became increasingly more radical, advocating nationalization of industries and limits on private property, a position the majority of the Argentine bishops would not tolerate. The Argentine experience was re-enacted by similar groups throughout Latin America.

In 1976 came a military coup in Argentina in which Western-backed terrorists, initially headed by General Jorge Rafael Videla, overthrew Isabelita, whose period in office combined brutality with total economic incompetence and raging inflation. The new dictator went on to massacre an estimated 30,000 people in a country of 40 million in what became known as 'the Dirty War'. Latin America was fast turning into a region of military dictatorship and horror. Stroessner, who, when he seized power, was an isolated dictatorial figure, found himself surrounded by sympathetic military figures in Brazil, Chile, Argentina, Bolivia and Uruguay, which saw elected governments ejected by generals. He was able to turn these developments to his advantage by helping to establish a scarcely disguised league of police states – all as a contribution to 'national security', a benefit that was never meant to be extended to the poorer members of society.

In Argentina much of the Church disgraced itself with its partiality for a series of military dictators such a Videla and those who followed him; other Catholics saw hope in the movements of the radical left.

In the spirit of Sigaud from Brazil, senior Argentine prelates had stood out in promoting the 1976 coup. One of the instigators was Victorio Manuel Bonamín, the second-ranking bishop to the forces, who preached at the popular pilgrimage place at Luján outside Buenos Aires in September 1975 and declared that the armed forces had a divine mission to rule Argentina. He also praised a military offensive against guerrillas in the northern province of Tucumán as a sacred crusade against communism. In words that would have suited the most extreme of twenty-first-century Islamist militants he said, 'How good it is to be able to say of [the military] that they are a phalanx of honest, spotless people who have ... purified themselves in a Jordan of blood to place themselves at the head of the country [to guide Argentina] to its great future destinies.'

Far from contradicting Bonamín, Archbishop Adolfo Tortolo, his superior as principal pastor to the forces, said that he 'was not in the least surprised by the contents of the homily'. Guillermo Bolatti, archbishop of Rosario, followed this up a few days later with a diatribe against democracy and 'the free play of political parties', which he claimed was responsible for 'the worst crisis in the country's history'. Moreover, said the archbishop in a sideswipe against such as the MSTM, the churches 'also have been incubating guerrillas'. Cardinal Juan Carlos Aramburu, archbishop of Buenos Aires, made the absurd claim at a mass in the capital's cathedral that the murderous Argentine police were 'benefactors of our society'.

On 5 August 1976, at the age of fifty-three, Angelelli was killed by Videla's assassins. The military, assured of the support of Argentine conservatives, business leaders and Western governments, did their best to hide the extent of the atrocities they were committing.

On the day of his death, Angelelli's car, driven by his secretary, was pushed off the highway at speed by supporters of General Videla, who had been in power in Buenos Aires for two years. A few days before his murder Angelelli had been investigating the torture and slow death on 18 July of two of his priests, Carlos Murias and Gabriel Longueville, who had been seized by unknown men and driven away in a car without number plates, their corpses dumped on a road two days later.

The bishop appears not to have died in the crash but to have been shot in the back of the head in what a judge, considering the death in 1986, said was not a traffic accident but 'a coldly premeditated homicide', as evidence collected on the spot had long pointed to. Directly after Angelelli's murder the Vatican newspaper *Osservatore Romano* referred to it as 'a strange accident', while Juan Carlos Aramburu, who had just been made a cardinal, mendaciously claimed, 'There are no concrete proofs to talk of a crime.'

Sadly Archbishop Pío Laghi, the papal nuncio also known to be close to Videla, with whom he regularly played tennis, vilified liberation theologians and in a magazine[3] published in Bologna in July 1997 claimed, 'What really happened in Argentina I only learned of when I was no longer there.' Such a claim was palpably mendacious, given the atrocities that the military regime committed and which were the subject of loud and agonized protests which could not have escaped the ears of any nuncio, however close to the regime to which he was accredited. Laghi, who died in 2009, went on from Argentina to become the papal representative in the USA in 1984 and seemed to take little exception to the policies of the Contra terrorists, or the USA and its allies in Central America during the Reagan years.

Jorge Novak was another prominent *Verbista* who maintained the good name of his order in the face of activity such as Laghi's. Novak was appointed bishop of Quilmes, an industrial suburb of Buenos Aires, in the year Angelelli was murdered, and was among the small group of bishops who made no secret of their opposition to Videla and his butchery. Novak's geographical position near the capital gave his words resonance at a time when the Argentine bishops and their leaders were, by their uncritical attitudes to the horrors perpetrated by the generals, covering themselves with the opprobrium into which they were to sink after the military dictatorship departed and their collaboration with its worst features was revealed.

Novak was a founder of the Ecumenical Movement for Human Rights. His book about the group's work, *Esto no es marxismo, es Evangelio* ('This is Not Marxism, This is the Gospel'), stood as a reproach to the many Argentine cardinals, bishops, clergy and lay people who had betrayed their calling in the face of military terrorism.

Fernando Lugo himself was growing up alongside the Paraná in a part of South America where two more *Verbistas* were setting him an excellent example of devotion to their faith.

Across the river from Encarnación, birthplace of Stroessner and near which Lugo himself was born, stands the Argentine city of Posadas. Posadas was the territory of a *Verbista* who was showing how a member of his order could rival Angelelli in devotion to duty. Jorge Kémérer had been ordained a priest of the SVD in 1932 when he was twenty-four. Twenty-four years later, in 1957, he was appointed bishop in Posadas.

---

3. *Il Regno*, 797.

From 1957 until his retirement in 1986, through various Argentine regimes and for most of the time Stroessner was in power across the river, the bishop devoted himself to the 700,000 people living in 30,000 square kilometres of one of the poorest parts of Argentina, 80 per cent of whom were deemed to be Catholics.

Kémérer was constantly worried by the paucity of clergy in his own diocese and throughout Latin America who were available to attend to the needs of the people. It was estimated in 1966 that there were 303,385 Catholics in the diocese, which had eighty-six priests to attend to their spiritual needs, an average of 3,527 people per priest.

Like other bishops in the region, he had the reputation of not being too harsh on those priests who fell short on the question of celibacy. His worry came out strongly in the words he delivered at Vatican II in October 1963. Speaking on the question of the re-establishment of married deacons who could take on some of the responsibilities of the clergy, a proposition on which the Council could not make up its mind, he intervened forcefully in favour of the idea. After a string of bishops had argued against any relaxation of celibacy, Kémérer addressed the gathering. He argued that to demand that deacons remain celibate would sink all hope of easing the dramatic shortage of personnel in Latin America. He wanted there to be deacons who would continue with their working life while helping their parishes at weekends. 'Canonically and theologically they would belong to the hierarchy, but psychologically and culturally to the people,' he said.

He finished with a powerful appeal for more flexible ways of thought.

> The restoration of the diaconate is our great hope; and it is the wish of many bishops in Latin America that you, Venerable Fathers, do not deprive us of this hope when the matter come[s] to the vote. The door is already open, and if among you there are some who do not wish to enter, we shall not force you to enter. But we graciously beg you not to close the door on us, because we do want to enter. Allow us to do so![4]

The assembly broke into applause and the point was won, though the battle for the routine admission of married men to the priesthood was not.

After Videla's 1976 putsch Kémérer was, with Angelelli, one of a

---

4. Kémérer speaking at Vatican II, 14 October 1963, quoted in Novak (1964: 125).

handful of Catholic leaders who distanced himself from the surrounding situation of terror and atrocity. He forbore to condemn the MSTM.

Unlike many Catholic leaders in Argentina, he bothered about human rights of individuals, instanced by the case of Mónica Beatriz Bustos. In April 1976 she was seized by the government and illegally imprisoned in the Posadas police headquarters where she was subjected to savage torture that left her in a coma for three days. She was saved by Kémérer's intervention; he succeeded in locating her despite the usual denials that the authorities used during the Dirty War that they did not have her.

Verbista influence on Lugo was strong and growing. Not only was the formidable Kémérer across the river in Posadas, in the future president's own home town one *Verbista* succeeded another as the young and ambitious Lugo grew up. Encarnación itself was at the time in ecclesiastical terms a 'territorial prelature', or something short of a full diocese. As such it could rely for funding on funds from Rome. The man in charge was Johannes Wiesen, a German. After twenty-two years as a *Verbista* priest Wiesen was appointed to run Encarnación as its prelate in January 1957, a few weeks before Kémérer was appointed bishop of Posadas. Wiesen was not consecrated a bishop until 1964, when his fellow *Verbista* came across the river from Posadas to join in his consecration.

At the age of fifty-seven Juan Bockwinkel, another German-born *Verbista*, took charge of Encarnación in succession to Wiesen in May 1968 when it was made into a full diocese – and had the responsibility of sustaining itself financially without counting on the Vatican's automatic assistance. Kémérer again came across the Paraná from Posadas to join in the consecration of a fellow member of his order. In 1970 Lugo became a novice of the Divine Word Missionaries.

ITAIPÚ: CONSTRUCTION AND CORRUPTION

At this time Stroessner was planning the lasting monument by which he wanted to be remembered. In one of the few inspirational ideas of his dictatorship he decided he was going to dam the Paraná river and take advantage of the energy its waters generated. He certainly played his part in creating something of great importance, which completely transformed not just the once neglected eastern part of the country but Paraguay as a whole. At the same time he entrenched the habit of corruption, which was to make the rich of Paraguay richer and widen the gap in wealth between his friends and the mass of the people. He also created problems that years later were to haunt Lugo as a politician.

Far larger than any other in the world until the arrival of the Three Gorges Dam in China, the Itaipú scheme harnessed the power of the slow-flowing River Paraná in a colossal civil engineering creation whose output of electricity had the ability to produce more energy than any other installation in the world.

The vast earth dam, 7.7 kilometres long and nearly 200 metres high, was built below a stupendous set of cataracts so remote and inaccessible that few people had ever had the chance of visiting them.

Cunninghame Graham quotes Félix de Azara in his history of Paraguay, published in Madrid in 1847, and his vivid description of the natural phenomenon, the Salto de Guayrá – or the Sete Quedas (Seven Falls) in Portuguese – which was the inspiration of the enormous work of civil engineering. The Spaniard called it 'a tremendous precipice of water worthy of Homer or of Virgil's pen'.

Cunninghame Graham continues:

> He says the waters do not fall vertically as from a balcony or a window, but by an inclined plane at an inclination of about fifty degrees. The river close to the top of the falls is about four thousand nine hundred Castilian yards in breadth, and suddenly narrows to about seventy yards and rushes over the fall with such terrific violence as if it wished to 'displace the centre of the earth ...' The dew or vapour which rises from the fall is seen in the shape of a column from many miles away, and on it hangs a perpetual rainbow, which trembles as the earth seems to tremble under one's feet.

Emmanuel de Bourgade la Dardye, writing in 1892, described the whirlpools that were produced as the river crashed over the rocks:

> The waters gather themselves in circular eddies whence they flow in falls varying from fifty to sixty feet in depth; these circular eddies, which are quite independent of one another, range along an arc of about two miles in its stretch. They are detached like cauldrons yawning unexpectedly at one's feet, in which the flood seethes with incredible fury; every one of these has opened for itself a narrow orifice in the rock, through which, like a stone from a sling, the water is hurled into the central whirlpool. The width of these outlets rarely exceeds fifteen yards, but their depth cannot be estimated. They all empty themselves into one central chamber about 200 feet wide, rushing into it with astounding velocity ... A more imposing spectacle can scarcely be conceived, and I doubt whether abysses such as these exist elsewhere in the world.

Such abysses no longer exist. It was possible to view the savage maelstrom from the air before the construction work began, a wild scene that contrasted astonishingly with the impressive sight forty years later of the harnessed waters of the Paraná pouring out from under the dam after they had done their work spinning the turbine to produce amazing amounts of electricity.

After his association with the Brazilian military dictatorship created the enormous hydroelectric dam at Itaipú, Stroessner subsequently created another, with Argentina, at Yacyretá. The former brought life and population to a part of a country that had not seen much of either. Its origins are to be found in his strategic ideas. One idea was that the vast areas of idle land in Paraguay should become productive through the establishment of state-aided settlements. A second idea, born perhaps of his training as a young officer with the Brazilian forces, was that his country should do more to free itself of undue reliance on Argentina, whose cities and port controlled landlocked Paraguay's connections with the outside world. Stroessner was reported as saying that without a stronger connection through Brazil to the Atlantic his country was 'a human being with only one lung'.

The Brazilians for their part, devoted to their centuries-old and successful doctrine of expanding their territory and influence to the west whenever the opportunity arose – a sort of more peaceful *Drang nach Westen* – were keen on the idea. President Juscelino Kubitschek, the Brazilian leader who bore most credit for the creation of the new capital of Brasília, financed a road from the border at Puerto Presidente Franco on the Paraná near the junction with the Iguazú to the Paraguayan town of Coronel Oviedo to provide a major road link to Paraguay's eastern neighbour.

Early in 1955 Captain Porfirio Pereira Ruiz Díaz was called into the office of the commander of the army's engineers. He was told he was to carve a road across the 200 kilometres that divided the town of Coronel Oviedo from the Paraná river farther to the east. Coronel Oviedo, lying 135 kilometres to the east of Asunción, was precariously linked to the capital by a road only half of which was surfaced. But the astonished Pereira was told that road-building plant had been bought – bulldozers and other earthmoving equipment, dump trucks and everything else necessary for the task of establishing the permanent link for traffic between Asunción and the border with Brazil. The thirty-year-old soldier had had a little experience, driving a road 30 kilometres north from Coronel Oviedo to the township of Carayaó, a task he and his men accomplished 'with picks and shovels and wheelbarrows'. His new task illustrates the degree of desolation Paraguay was living in during Lugo's early years.

Recalling the scene in *ABC Color*,[5] Pereira recalled how at the time Coronel Oviedo 'was to all intents and purposes where Paraguay ended. Thereafter it was bush, bush and more bush.' The new road would be the first in the country to be constructed with advanced construction equipment. He and his men were to be given a month's training to master the new machines with a private company, which itself knew little more than the army did about how to manoeuvre a bulldozer.

For two years he and his First Engineer Battalion pushed on, chasing bandits out of the occasional settlements they came across in a largely uninhabited wilderness, bridging watercourses, righting the equipment that fell into the streams, putting up with tropical days with their mosquitoes and poisonous animals and freezing nights, not forgetting the constant threat of leishmaniasis, a disease transmitted by a parasite deposited by a sandfly which produces repulsive ulcers, boils and disfigurement, and which is still widespread in Paraguay.

They reached the Paraná in February 1957, and a month later, on the feast of St Blaise, the patron saint of Paraguay, a new town was inaugurated at a place whose original name had been Puerto Miseria, 'Port Poverty'. The foundation stone was laid of the new Puerto Presidente Stroessner. It was so remote from Asunción that the guests at the inauguration came by air, landing across the river at the Brazilian airport at Foz de Iguaçú. More than four centuries after the foundation of Asunción by the Spaniards in 1537 there was a connection between Paraguay and its neighbour to the east.

The impending construction of the new bridge, the provision of two petrol pumps and the building of a charmless concrete cavern of a casino were designed to attract Brazilian tourists from the town of Foz de Iguaçú on the opposite bank which was already established as the best point for visitors to view the Iguazú Falls. The activity was soon bringing in settlers who set about the backbreaking task of clearing the forest round about. Food was scarce and initially had to be flown in from other parts of the country.

Yet soon the place was booming, despite the lack of effective town planning, its unsurfaced streets, ankle deep in the region's red mud, and general air of chaotic confusion.[6] Little plots of land were provided to humble people while those with influence were able to get themselves assigned large areas. Traders appeared from Asunción or over the river from Brazil, together with some whose fathers and grandfathers had

---

5. *ABC Color*, 24 October 2008.
6. Neri (2003: *passim*).

made money downstream in Encarnación in the traditional trading in human beings of both sexes. Smallholders knew where they could find an accessible market for whatever food they grew.

The road connection across the Paraná was finalized when the Puente de la Amistad, the Friendship Bridge, was inaugurated on 27 March 1965 by Stroessner and Marshal Castelo Branco, the Brazilian officer who had helped to overthrow Brazil's civilian government the previous year.

By 1972 the population had reached 7,069; ten years later it stood at 49,423. In 1992 there were 133,823 inhabitants and the population was soon exceeding 200,000. After Stroessner's fall it was renamed unimaginatively Ciudad del Este, 'The City of the East'.

At the same time President Kubitschek and his civilian successors Jânio Quadros and João Goulart were thinking hard about the best way for Brazil to tap the energy of the falls for itself. The USSR, Japan and the USA were all interested in helping to finance and build such a scheme. Yet the Paraguayan side learnt of the scheme only through a newspaper report in 1962. Each side had the idea that the falls lay in its territory, the Paraguayans arguing that their title went back to 1525 and had been confirmed in treaties between Spain and Portugal, then the colonial power in Brazil, in 1757 and 1777. In January 1964, less than three months before his overthrow by the military, Goulart welcomed Stroessner to his ranch in the Pantanal area of Brazil and the two agreed that the best way forward would be a joint enterprise to harness the waters of the Paraná. The military coup against Goulart on 1 March did not help matters.

By June 1965, a few weeks after the inauguration of the bridge, there was tension between soldiers of the two countries stationed on the border: for a few hours a Brazilian army sergeant detained a high-level Paraguayan delegation visiting the site at Puerto Renato until his orders were countermanded by his captain. At the England–Paraguay World Cup qualifying match in Asunción enthusiastic Paraguayan fans raised a banner visible on television bearing the message 'Los Saltos del Guairá son Paraguayos', 'The Guairá Falls are Paraguayan', which was pulled down by the police on Stroessner's direct orders. The antipathy that many Paraguayans felt towards their giant neighbours to the east, rooted in ancient memories of the seventeenth-century slave-hunting expeditions of the *bandeirantes* in the reductions and the defeat of López by Brazil in the War of the Triple Alliance in the nineteenth century, were always present and sometimes patent.

In the end the two sides came back to the view that the best way forward was by mutual agreement, and in June 1966 the two dictator-

8 Itaipú dam from the eastern (Brazilian) bank of the Paraná River.

ships, in a formal agreement signed by their foreign ministers, agreed on the joint exploitation of the hydroelectric resources of the cataract. Each would have the right to half the power and could not export it to any other country without the permission of the other, a stipulation that adversely affected Paraguay, which could not use its share, but not Brazil, whose expanding economy could not get enough electric power.

Years of engineering studies came to a climax in April 1973 when Stroessner and the Brazilian dictator General Emílio Garrastazú Médici witnessed their foreign ministers signing the Treaty of Itaipú, which regulated the joint use of the hydroelectric potential of the river.

In May of the following year, near the site of the future Itaipú dam, Stroessner and General Ernesto Geisel, who had succeeded Médici as dictator of Brazil, witnessed the signing of the document that created the Entidad Binacional Itaipú, EBI, or the Itaipú Binational Entity, charged with building and running the great scheme. The details of the bilateral agreement were kept secret, but it was confirmed that the financial burden would be carried mainly by the Brazilians.

Itaipú was to generate 12,600 megawatts using eighteen giant turbine units. Nine of them were, according to the EBI,[7] to produce power at the 50-hertz frequency used in Paraguay, while the other nine were to

7. www.itaipu.gov.py.

generate at Brazil's 60-hertz frequency. The plant began to be commissioned in 1984 but was not fininshed till 1991, two years after the dictator's overthrow.

The work to complete Itaipú was Herculean. In 1975 a diversion channel was dug to take the water out of the way of the engineers who started building the dam. In 1982 the completed sluice gates were closed and the reservoir began to fill. The first giant section of a turbine arrived in March 1982 and the first electricity was produced two years later.

The project had involved the excavation of eight and a half times more material than was dug out to build the Channel Tunnel, and the line of dump trucks needed to carry it away would have stretched for 128,000 kilometres or three times round the earth. For every cubic metre of concrete used in the Tunnel fifteen cubic metres were used at Itaipú. That would have been enough to build a city the size of Rio de Janeiro or 210 football stadiums the size of the Maracanã, that city's pride and joy. The iron and steel used would have been enough to build 380 Eiffel Towers. Each one of the turbines is as high as an eight-storey building and weighs 6,600 tons. Each one could in 1999 supply four times the electricity that was being used in Asunción. The designers produced 1,200,000 drawings, which, if piled one on top of the other, would have reached as high as a 50-storey skyscraper. The EBI[8] said the dam held back a reservoir that measured 1,350 square kilometres and contained 29 billion square metres of muddy water.

In the turbine hall today the engineers cycle up and down deep in the concrete under the silent, dimly lit arches of the dam, which give the structure the air of some modern cathedral. Nothing is heard but a gentle hum as 16,000 cubic metres of water a second spin the turbines producing the electric current. The water escapes into the spillways in plumes of spray and a rainbow and settles down to resume its jouney to the River Plate and the southern Atlantic Ocean 1,000 kilometres distant.

In 1973 Stroessner witnessed the signing of a similar agreement with the Argentines, now being ruled for a second time by the aged Juan Domingo Perón, for the construction of a jointly owned dam, Yacyretá, downstream from Itaipú on the Paraná at a point where the river marked the boundary between the two countries. It was not destined to have the effect that Itaipú was destined to have, and was not completed for many years, but it eventually did raise water levels in the city of Stroessner's birth and Lugo's boyhood, Encarnación.

---

8. www.itaipu.gov.py.

WAR WITH STROESSNER

As corruption flowed unchecked in Paraguayan society and Lugo committed himself to the *Verbista*, Stroessner took a harder line with the Church. Since the start of his presidency he had dispatched any domestic political challenge, comprehensively sidelined the Liberals and cemented a close relationship with the USA. The only remaining irritant to his rule was the Church, which showed no sign of retreating from its opposition to him. He determined that it, too, had to be brought to obedience.

As the Agrarian Leagues grew in strength, government troops began to harass the settlements where their power lay. The bloodiest intervention came in 1975 at Jejuí, 200 miles north-east of Asunción, where twenty-four families were besieged by seventy soldiers after the government charged that the community was the headquarters of a guerrilla unit. Two French priests, a Spanish nun, two US citizens who were leading figures in the US Catholic Relief Service, a Paraguayan deacon and five peasants were seized. The local priest, Braulio Maciel, was shot in the leg and repeatedly beaten, and when the nun tried to intervene on Maciel's behalf, she, too, was beaten. That same week a Trinidadian priest, an Italian clergyman and two Paraguayan deacons were arrested during a military round-up of peasants in ten other communities. Repeated efforts by the local bishop, Marichevich, to reach Jejuí were prevented, his life was threatened and he was told that Pastor Coronel, chief of police investigations, had declared him *persona non grata*.

The community's fields, houses and livestock were destroyed. The soldiers also stole the equivalent of US$7,000 which had been donated by European Catholic organizations for peasants to buy land.

As the Church newspaper *Sendero* ('The Path') pointed out, no guerrillas or guns were found at the colony, only Bibles and peasant prayer books and 'a priest whose mission is to pardon'. 'Forgive them, Father, for they know not what they do,' cried Father Maciel after they shot him. 'These communities' only crime is that they are Christian,' stated the Paraguayan bishops in a joint statement at the time.

In 1976 the violence of the dictatorship was again challenged by an effort to set up a viable guerrilla movement, the OPM or Military Political Movement, consisting at its peak of some four hundred supporters who brought out a newspaper, *Tata pirirí* (Guaraní for 'creeping fire'). It did not last long. On 3 April 1976 one of its leaders, Carlos Brañas, was picked up by Stroessner's secret police as he arrived in Asunción from Posadas bearing secret documents. Following his torture, other members of the OPM were detained in the capital. There were two

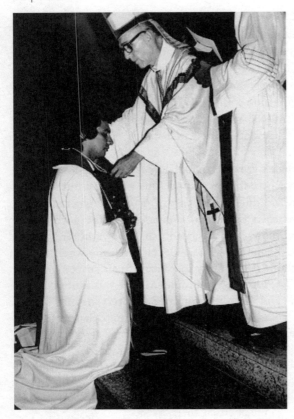

9 Lugo ordained priest, August 1977.

armed clashes on the two subsequent days in which OPM members and a policeman were killed and another policeman injured.

Two of the group, Mario Schaerer, hit by a bullet in the leg, and his wife, Guillermina Kanonikov, sought refuge in the church of San Cristóbal, where the priest in charge, Raimundo Roy, a French-Canadian, handed them over to the police. Schaerer died under torture, though his wife survived and returned to active politics. Roy had to undergo psychological counselling when he finally understood the consequences of his actions.

As all this was going on, and at a low point of Stroessner's relations with the Church, Lugo was preparing for the priesthood. He took his vows of perpetual fidelity to the SVD and went to study for a degree at the Nuestra Señora de la Asunción Catholic University in the capital, where he obtained a bachelor's degree in religious sciences. He was ordained a priest on 15 August 1977 and the next year went off to Ecuador. There events were to change his life and make him a practitioner of liberation theology of the sort which many in Rome, not least John Paul II, had no use for.

A BISHOP IN A PONCHO

In the High Andes Lugo saw – as Bishop Bartolomé de Las Casas had seen more than four and a half centuries before – the wretched lives of the Indians, once part of a proud empire, now reduced to beggary and hunger by the descendants of the Spanish conquistadors armed with the gospel, firearms and that weapon hitherto unknown in the continent of America, the horse.

Lugo's time in Ecuador, where the majority are indigenous, put him under the spell of the bishop of Riobamba, Leonidas Proaño, one of the leading South American *liberacionistas*. 'We young priests were engaged mainly on youth work. But we were constantly going to talk to the man they called the bishop in the poncho or the bishop of the Indians,' he recalled in an interview for this book. The parallels with his country and its Guaranís were never far from his mind.

He remembered the big clash in Riobamba between radical clergy and a dim military junta. It was a perfect illustration of the antipathy that separated those in the Church who wanted change from the generals, who, under the coaching of Western powers, acted to protect an indefensible status quo. What was at issue was the so-called National Security Doctrine – a charter for the security of right-wing military dictators rather than the security of the population – which was much in vogue in the western hemisphere at the time.

On 12 August 1976, a year or so before Lugo's arrival in Ecuador, the junta had seized Proaño and sixteen foreign bishops. They included Vicente Zazpe, archbishop of the Argentine diocese of Santa Fe and leader of the progressive Argentine bishops, and four from the USA, including Archbishop Robert Fortune Sanchez of Santa Fe. They were replying to an invitation from Proaño to a gathering in a retreat centre to discuss pastoral matters. The military considered it subversive. A government minister sent forty police officers to seize them and a group of seventy priests and laypeople, including Adolfo Pérez Esquivel, who was to be awarded the Nobel Peace Prize in 1980 for his defiance of the terrorism of the Argentine military during the Dirty War.

As Bishop Mariano Parra León, a sixty-five-year-old Venezuelan, recounted to the US journalist Penny Lernoux, who was writing for the New York-based Alicia Patterson Foundation, the group was midway through a meeting in Riobamba on pastoral questions when '40 barbarians armed with machine guns, revolvers and tear gas bombs burst in on us. None of us was allowed to touch any of our personal belongings, not even to put on a pair of socks. We were pushed at gunpoint into a waiting bus, 80 of us crammed into a space meant for 50.'

After a three-hour trip through the Andes in the dark, the bishops were locked up in the San Gregorio Prison in Quito, without food and sleeping on the floor. As a result of the commotion, Bishop Parra had a heart attack. The papal nuncio, Archbishop Luigi Accogli, visited them in the early hours of the morning, though Pablo Muñoz Vega, the Jesuit cardinal who was archbishop of Quito, did not visit.

After putting them all under arrest, the junta expelled the sixteen in an action that reflected worse on the members of the Ecuadorean military than on the bishops. As if to underline the hostility between the region's military and the Church, or at least its progressive wing, General Pinochet, the dictator of Chile whose intelligence agents had been at work in Quito, where he himself had once been sent to help establish a military academy, organized his supporters to throw stones at the three Chilean bishops at Santiago airport as they eventually found their way home. The crowd carried placards with slogans such as 'Filthy priests', 'Sons of Marxism', 'Corrupt priests' and 'Priests yes, Activists no'. The Chilean press, notably *El Mercurio, La Segunda* and *Crónica*, owned by the Edwards family, the principal cheerleaders of the dictator in Chile and the USA, inveighed against 'left-wing clericalism' and its 'arrogant extremism'.

'I was proud that one of the bishops detained in Riobamba by the military was Paraguayan, Mgr Bogarín Argaña,' Lugo commented. At the time of the arrest Ramón Pastor Bogarín was bishop of the Paraguayan diocese of San Juan Bautista de las Misiones: the sixty-five-year-old, who had been a strong supporter of the Christian Agrarian Leagues, died on 3 September 1976, less than a month after his release by the Ecuadorean junta.

His record of defiance to Stroessner had made him a national figure. Frequently threatened by the police, Bogarín was for years in the vanguard of the battle. According to Penny Lernoux, the US journalist, church people told her he would have been named archbishop of Asunción had the Vatican not given in during the 1950s to Stroessner's demands for his removal from the capital. Bogarín had incurred official wrath while auxiliary bishop of Asunción because of his work among workers and students, and in 1957 the Church installed him in the newly created diocese of San Juan Bautista. But he would not be silenced. Soon large landowners in the region were complaining about his work among the peasants.

'They sent the local police chief to kill me, but when I confronted him he didn't have the courage to shoot,' Bogarín told Lernoux shortly before his death. 'The government makes a serious mistake in believing that my death will end the Church's criticisms. I am only one of 12 bishops, and all of us are united in our opposition to the government. My death will change nothing.'

Five thousand peasants attended his funeral in defiance of military checkpoints and police suspension of all transport in the area.

Lugo summed up his time in the Andes in an interview for this book. 'If I hadn't gone to Ecuador I wouldn't be the person I am today.'

At the same time as the Church and Stroessner were beginning to fall out, there were positive developments in his relationship with the USA, which began to move into its most intimate phase.

In August 1957 Admiral Ageton was replaced by Walter Ploeser as US ambassador and as an expediter of financial aid to Stroessner, including loans for the telephone service and for the remodelling of the international airport. Ploeser also persuaded the First National City Bank to set up in the Paraguayan capital.

Eisenhower did one last favour for Stroessner when he sent his vice-president, Richard Nixon, to Asunción in May 1958. The visit went well enough, being criticized more in the press of surrounding countries than it was by the controlled press in Paraguay itself. Nixon was effusive in his praise for the tyrant: 'In the field of international affairs, I do not know of any other nation which has risen more strongly than yours against the threat of communism and this is one reason why I feel especially happy to be here.'[9]

Meanwhile, on the military front, Washington was seeking an ambitious strategic objective by promoting the idea of 'national security', which posited that the main threat to Latin America came not from outside the region but from inside it in the persons of those who wanted to overturn the established order. Security had to be ensured for the status quo, which demanded the preservation of the standards of living of the very richest members of society and the maintenance of the gross social inequalities that had been patent since the arrival of the Europeans on the continent. In succeeding years this supposed 'national security' doctrine was embraced by the Latin American military with an enthusiasm that was fostered by successive US governments, which made sure that the most enthusiastic of them benefited from weapons and training delivered at cut price. Pursuing the idea first put forward in the

9. Quoted in Livingstone (2009: 66).

times of President Harry Truman at the end of the Second World War, Washington strategists argued that Latin American armies should not see loyalty to their own governments as paramount but should adhere to the idea of the protection of 'Western Christian civilization', a term used by right-wing propagandists in Washington and Latin America when referring to the USA and its allies.

The list of those held to oppose 'Western Christian civilization' – a term that became very popular with Latin American military dictators – was to be carefully prepared and presented in the State Department and the Pentagon and feature prominently reformists, social democrats, communists – where they existed – and all others who were critical of US political strategies in the western hemisphere as the undesirables.

After the victory of Castro in 1959 the USA set up the Alliance for Progress, whose aim, according to the Kennedy administration, was to stop 'the virus of Castro from spreading contagion throughout the region', but which, according to Noam Chomsky, writing in 1986, was 'totally cynical'. Referring to its results on the beef industry in Central America, which the US government was keen to promote, Chomsky pointed out[10] that while the production of beef rose, the local consumption of beef fell:

> The reason was that croplands that had been used for subsistence crops for the population [were] being eliminated in favour of grazing lands for wealthy ranchers tied to American agribusiness who were producing beef for export. In fact, throughout this period while there was statistical growth, there was also increased misery and increased starvation.

Something similar was taking place in Paraguay. A US Agency for International Development assessment of the Alliance for Progress in Paraguay claimed that 'Major USAID efforts were devoted to developing the institutional capabilities of the various ministries and agencies within the Government of Paraguay. Special emphasis was placed on developing the capabilities of the tax and census offices.'

In reality there was no objective evidence that the 'Alliance', which died around 1973, brought any improvement in the conduct of government during the dictatorship or in the years of Colorado rule after the overthrow of Stroessner. When Lugo came to power in 2008 the spasmodic efforts of some in authority to introduce income tax had

---

10. Noam Chomsky, 'The empire and ourselves', *A Solidarity Pamphlet*, 9 April 1986.

been comprehensively stifled by those on whom it would have been imposed.

An important concrete product of the 'national security' ideas to halt the influence of Fidel Castro was the School of the Americas (SOA), established by President J. F. Kennedy in the Panama Canal Zone, which over the decades taught generations of Paraguayan and other Latin American officers the US view of the world. Paraguayan officers, among 60,000 alumni, were welcome there, rubbing shoulders with dictators such as General Hugo Banzer of Bolivia and Leopoldo Galtieri and Roberto Viola of Argentina. The young Lugo was to grow up in a country over which the shadow of the School of the Americas very definitely fell. It was later revealed that it had done much to refine the skills of police and military torturers.

SOA graduates were responsible for the massacres in the banana plantations in the Urabá region of Colombia and the assassination of Lugo's hero Oscar Romero, archbishop of San Salvador, in 1980, the El Mozote massacre of 900 civilians in 1981, and the killing of Elba Ramos, her fourteen-year-old daughter Celina and six Jesuit priests in El Salvador in 1989.

Among the most notorious Paraguayan officers at the SOA in 1956 was Alejandro Fretes Dávalos. By 1976 he had been promoted to general and was chief of the general staff, with a particular interest in intelligence. He was a key figure in the establishment of Operation Cóndor, which coordinated the smooth collaboration of the military dictatorships of Brazil, Uruguay and Argentina, arresting, imprisoning, torturing and kidnapping their opponents. Paraguay joined in July 1976.

The first major victory of this 'national security' strategy came when Lugo was a young teenager. It took the form of the overthrow of the reformist civilian government of Brazil in 1964 by a group of generals who were over the subsequent decade and a half to preserve the status quo by a series of spoof elections backed up by liberal use of torture and terror. Western European powers took no exception to the dictatorship in a country that was a particularly good customer for weapons, and General Ernesto Geisel, dictator from 1974 to 1979, was even accommodated at Buckingham Palace in London during a state visit to Queen Elizabeth.

Meanwhile Stroessner had the chance to make a reality of his promises to Eisenhower. He sent Paraguayan troops to back the US invasion of the Dominican Republic in 1965. This was staged by Washington after patriotic Dominican officers looked as though they had a chance of success in overthrowing a military junta and restoring the constitutionally elected president, Juan Bosch, whom the junta had overthrown in 1963.

Lyndon Johnson told the world that the patriots were communists. Some 42,000 US Marines, allied to a handful of Paraguayan troops, attacked the constitutionalist forces and unsurprisingly won, plunging the country back into the poverty and torpor from which Bosch had tried to pull it. Colonel Roberto Cubas Barboza, who had been an important figure in helping Stroessner in his successful bid for power in 1953, commanded the Paraguayan contingent. Despite – or perhaps because of – the high marks he received from the US military, the dictator dismissed him from the army on his return and sent him into internal exile. He later died in an aircraft accident.

As thanks for his help in conquering the Dominican Republic in 1965, Stroessner received his reward. Having engineered a new term as president on 19 February 1968, he was invited to Washington and a meeting with President Lyndon Johnson on 9 March.

This encounter, however, was to turn out to mark the high point of relations between the rulers in Asunción and Washington. Johnson was succeeded by Richard Nixon in January 1969. Thinking to maintain the relationship that he had started when Eisenhower had sent him to Paraguay in 1968, Nixon dispatched Nelson Rockefeller to Asunción a few months later. This time, with riots against Vietnam involvement spreading over North America and Europe, the US envoy was received with extreme hostility by students and schoolchildren.

Nixon's passion was to fight the trade in narcotics such as marijuana, cocaine and heroin while leaving the trade in mainstream drugs such as alcohol and tobacco alone. And Stroessner committed the imprudence of trying to protect a French adventurer and narcotics dealer, Joseph-Auguste Ricord. He had arrived in Paraguay from Buenos Aires in 1967, obtained Paraguayan nationality and started what became a popular bar and restaurant in the capital, the París Niza, from where he continued the trafficking of narcotics to the USA which he had started in Argentina. Four years later the US authorities sought to have him extradited to their country. They initially failed, Stroessner blocking the extradition of a Paraguayan citizen in fear that the information he could provide about leading Paraguayans' involvement in the trade could harm his regime. But US agents went on to mount an unsuccessful attempt to kidnap him. It took the White House until August 1972 and a visit from an envoy carrying a letter to Stroessner from Nixon to get its hands on him, but he was eventually sent to the USA, where he received a twenty-year jail sentence.

Nixon's successor, Jimmy Carter, who succeeded him in 1977, invited the dictator to the White House, but the two ended up disliking each other as heartily as Eisenhower and he had got on well. US aid dried up and Stroessner tried to argue that the US leader was a communist. As the cold war began to wind down, the Paraguayan was increasingly seen in Washington as an international embarrassment. Relations were not aided by the appointment by Carter of Robert White as envoy to Paraguay. For the first time the US embassy began to maintain relations with the opposition, a move that infuriated Stroessner, who had it put about that not just the US head of state but his ambassador, who served from 1977 to 1980, was in league with the communists. He also put it about that White was an alcoholic. White, who was on hand to see the US Congress halt military aid to Paraguay (and Guatemala, El Salvador and Brazil) in 1978, continued to criticize the dictatorship after he left Asunción.

ASSASSINATION ON THE STREETS

The assassination in the streets of Asunción in September 1980 of General Anastasio 'Tachito' Somoza, the former dictator of Nicaragua, who had found refuge in Paraguay from the Sandinistas who had expelled him, gave Stroessner a chance to demonstrate to the world that the Paraguayan police were enthusiastic in putting into practice the lessons they had learned from Eisenhower's emissary, Colonel Thierry.

The Nicaraguan was being driven along Generalísimo Francisco Franco Avenue in his Mercedes-Benz at 10 a.m. when it was hit by a bazooka. But the police did not catch the assassin. He was Enrique Gorriarán Merlo, an Argentine revolutionary and one of the founders of the People's Revolutionary Army (ERP), with long experience of guerrilla violence. Gorriarán claimed[11] that he led the hit squad that, on instructions from the Sandinista security service, slipped into the Paraguayan capital, Asunción, and used his weapon to destroy Somoza's armour-plated car.

The Argentine evaded capture, though one member of the group, Alfredo Hugo Irurzun, was found and tortured to death. The nine torturers responsible for his death were still alive in November 2008, according to a publication of the small Febrerista Party published in that month. Stroessner, however, wanted to find more culprits, any culprits.

How he went about doing this is described in the book *La Sociedad Cautiva* ('The Captive Society'), written in 1987 by Heriberto Alegre for

11. Obituary, *Independent*, 26 September 2006.

the Paraguayan Committee for the Defence of Human Rights. It carries the account of a Chilean journalist, Rafael Mella Latorre, of his treatment by the authorities after he and his pregnant wife, María Cristina, were detained on 30 October 1980 some seven weeks after Somoza's assassination. The two were initially taken to police headquarters in Asunción, where they were separated. Mella was interviewed by Chief Inspector Alberto Cantero and Inspector Bazán, and thereafter put into a very crowded cell which contained a blocked toilet.

At dusk the following day, in the bathroom, his feet were tied to a ring in the floor, his hands manacled behind his back, and the guards pushed him underwater and threw water at him when he emerged. 'I thought my lungs would burst,' Mella said. The water torture was repeated several times. On one occasion during the torture he was given 'the thermometer', a copper cylinder which was pushed up his anus and connected to an electric current whose strength could be varied. Another day he was kept in a small wooden box, which forced him to adopt the foetal position for a whole day. 'When they let me out the pain was such that I screamed,' he said. On another occasion he was for several days put in 'the parking space', where there was room only to stand.

The following day Pastor Coronel, head of the investigations department, confirmed that his wife had lost her child and told him that she would receive medical attention if he signed a confession. 'It's up to you,' said Coronel, 'if you sign your wife's life will be saved. If you don't one dead woman won't cause any problems.'

Mella decided to sign on the spot and was allowed to see María Cristina for a few moments before she was taken off to hospital. Later that day he was told to write his life story and include the contacts he had had in planning Somoza's assassination. When he said he had no names to give he was told to invent them, which he did. The account was presented in court four years later. The case first went to a military commission of inquiry consisting of three generals, who found that he had had nothing to do with the killing.

At the end of April 1981 he was transferred to a police prison, where until October 1983 he was kept in an underground cell 1.25 metres high with a floor area of 1.8 metres by 60 centimetres. It had neither light nor a mattress, and his clothing consisted of skimpy underpants and a hand towel. Every third day food was pushed under the door, and he had a powdered milk can for his urine and faeces which he could push out only when it was full. He was continuously lice-ridden. When, after two and a half years, representatives of the International Committee of the

Red Cross were allowed to see him in 1983 they had to wait a day while the hair was shaved from his body so that the lice could be removed. On 21 June 1984 he was visited by a delegation from America's Watch, and the next day taken to the main prison of Asunción at Tacumbú. After five years, five months and ten days of detention, Mella was put on trial and given a six-year jail sentence as an accessory to Somoza's murder.

When in June 1986, as a private citizen, former ambassador White accompanied Domingo Laíno, the Liberal and a senior figure in the opposition who had been forbidden to return to his country, on a flight from Buenos Aires to Asunción, he received his own share of the police violence that awaited the arrival of the plane.

As the terror campaign progressed, Stroessner did not want remaining in the country an acute young clergyman who not only showed no sign of attachment to this government but who also was a close relative of Epifanio Méndez, whom he still feared was active in Asunción. His order had set Lugo the task of training the younger men who sought to become *Verbistas* and passing on to them the lessons he had brought from Ecuador. Stroessner therefore made it known to Lugo's superiors that they should send him out of the country. The dictatorship had already complained of the 'subversive content' of his sermons.

For its part the order, conscious of Stroessner's worries, gave their bright, high-flying young priest with some missionary and parish experience new opportunities. In 1983 he was sent to study at the Jesuits' Gregorian University in Rome for another degree in spirituality and sociology, with a specialization in the Church's social doctrine. A photograph taken in the Vatican shows Lugo with blossoming moustache and beard in his black clothes and clerical collar about to shake hands with John Paul II in a cassock of papal white.

The course demanded some familiarity with English, so in the middle of his studies he was dispatched to England on an eight-week intensive course at a language school in Soho Square, living at his order's house in north-west London. 'I enjoyed being in a cosmopolitan city like London. At the weekend I helped out saying masses at parishes near the house. But', he confessed wryly in an interview for this book, 'my English was virtually unintelligible. I spent time with the Latin Americans in the city.' He was a visitor at the Anglo-Paraguayan Society in London, where his compatriots gathered for social evenings and Paraguayan music.

STROESSNER CONFRONTS WASHINGTON

In February 1987 Clyde Taylor, the new US ambassador appointed by President Reagan, was attacked by Stroessner's men. Taylor, who served from the end of 1985 to September 1988, went to a lunch arranged by a group of opposition women in a private house to honour him in recognition of his action in favour of their cause, and a group of opponents of the government gathered in front of the house to shout anti-Stroessner slogans. The police made no secret of their unhappiness with this situation, adopting a hostile attitude to the guests, including foreign diplomats, as they arrived. While the hundred guests were present Stroessner's men peppered the house with tear-gas grenades. US diplomatic staff were among those physically affected, and in the end the US Marine Corps guards at the embassy were summoned to evacuate them. A strong State Department protest went off the next day. For his part Augusto Sabino Montanaro, the interior minister and landowner, exulted that he had Colorado (red) bombs to protect a Colorado government.

By the time Taylor's spell as ambassador was up, the dictator was abandoned by the US government and agencies which had done so much to support him. Now they were transferring their critical support elsewhere.

Back in Asunción in 1987 after four years in Rome and a second degree, Lugo started lecturing in theology at his old university, and soon his reputation grew. The years when Lugo was beginning to be more and more noticed in Paraguay were bad ones for Stroessner.

The Paraguayan bishops appointed him to their commission on doctrine and the Latin American Bishops Conference asked the new graduate from the Gregorian University to join their team concerned with theological reflection. Influenced by Proaño's liberation theology, he was getting to be known in Church circles continent-wide. Lugo was in a good position to observe the dictator.

It was General Andrés Rodríguez, whose son was married to the dictator's daughter, who threw Stroessner out on 3 February 1989 in a bloody coup. Scores died in battles between the Presidential Escort Battalion, allied to the police loyal to the dictator, and the tanks of Rodríguez's First Army Corps. Tension had been growing between the two men, with Rodríguez making no secret of his impatience to take over the presidency from the old man. When Stroessner confiscated his Guaraní money-exchange operation the gloves came off. The day after the fighting, he was sent off to his gilded exile in Brazil.

5 | THE RISE OF LUGO

General Andrés Rodríguez, the forceful son of an engine driver, was the US choice for the succession despite the information it possessed about his immense ill-gotten wealth and his corrupt practices. The US embassy had publicly said he was mixed up in drugs, but Rodríguez slapped the diplomats down and told them not to interfere in the country's internal affairs. One of the richest men in the country from his narcotics trafficking, he also owned large ranches, Munich, the biggest brewery, the Guaraní chain of currency exchange shops, an import-export business and a copper wire company. This fortune was amassed, as the *New York Times* recalled tartly in the obituary it published after his death on 22 April 1997, on the basis of army pay of US$500 a month.

But the general was seen in Washington as the man who could help the US retreat from its traditional support for dictators in Latin America. Yet in easing out the old tyrant, Rodríguez might be relied upon to do little or nothing to alter the social system in ways displeasing to US interests. And so it turned out.

To the surprise of many, Rodríguez, who assumed a provisional presidency, decreed a relaxation of the barriers to parliamentary practice which Stroessner had built up so carefully in his thirty-five years in power. Rodríguez, who had faithfully supported Stroessner's dictatorship over the decades and had upheld his offensive against the Church, decreed 'the start of the democratization of Paraguay, respect for Human Rights and the defence of our Roman Catholic Christian religion'.

The Congress elected by Stroessner fraudulently in 1988 was abolished and new elections were called for 1 May 1989. All political parties, except the communists, were allowed to organize and present candidates. Having hinted at what he might do, he put himself forward as a presidential candidate to serve out what remained of Stroessner's presidential term. He won with 75.9 per cent of the votes to the 19.4 per cent said to have been won by the indecisive veteran Liberal Laíno. No one was surprised that the elections were manipulated according to the well-tried systems of vote buying and rigging of the electoral rolls. Rodríguez stepped down in 1993.

In 1992, with Stroessner toppled and Rodríguez in power, the *Verbistas* named Lugo as head of their order in Paraguay a century after the first *Verbistas* had arrived in the country. He had achieved a position in the Church and there was no Stroessner there to block what he wanted to do.

CORRUPTION REVEALED

One part of Paraguayan life which was a constant concern for Lugo, and a factor that in his view stopped Paraguay being looked on as a 'serious' country, was corruption, and in the aftermath of the dictator's overthrow more and more material leaked out about the extent of bribery and financial swindles. Some of it concerned his fellow Christians and some those who merely sailed under Christian colours. As his experience of the politics of his country increased over the years, Lugo became convinced that corruption was at the heart of Stroessner's control of the population, rewarding those who supported him and keeping the majority in something approaching servitude. Consequently he concentrated his criticisms on corruption when he was a bishop, during his campaign for the presidency and from his first moments in office.

During the Stroessner dictatorship it was an open secret that he and his cronies had built up incalculable fortunes on the basis of bribes, the extortion of foreign investors and participation in siphoning of money from public institutions, direct robbery of the public purse, remittances from the government of Taiwan for the anti-communist campaign in Latin America, the laundering of money, and the smuggling of cars, cigarettes, alcohol, electronic articles and other illegal products. Court documents pertaining to charges made on his estate after Stroessner's death show that the money traced to the late dictator and his family totalled some $3,000 million. These figures tally with those prepared by Martín Almada, a notable opponent of Stroessner, and others who sought to recover assets stolen by the dictator. Almada himself lodged a claim against the Stroessner estate for a modest 500 million guaranies (some £72,000) in respect of the killing of his wife Celestina (she was subjected to recordings of the cries of her husband as he was being tortured) and of the injuries he suffered at Stroessner's hands.

The Stroessner family fortune came from landholdings, apartments, bank accounts in the USA, Europe and the Caribbean, hotels in the Brazilian town of Foz de Iguaçú, and real estate in the Buenos Aires districts of Caballito, Liniers, Flores and Morón. Then there were shares in shipping and insurance companies in Brazil and gold and diamond mines in South Africa.

One of the Stroessner family's solidest sources of finance was Taiwan, whose government Paraguay recognized in 1957 and which he visited for the first time in 1975, when he was received by the newly installed President Yen Chia-ken, who took over in that year on the death of Generalissimo Chiang Kai-shek. Chiang, the former leader of the Kuomintang army on the Chinese mainland, had ruled the island as head of state since 1950 after his forces were beaten by the communists and expelled to the island where he lived under the strategic protection of US forces. Yen introduced him to executives of the International Commercial Bank of China (ICBC), the successor to the long-established Bank of China, whose roots went back to the finance arm of the imperial court of the Ching Dynasty.

ICBC was charged with sending Stroessner cash for 'anti-communist activities' in Latin America. Stroessner became active in the World Anti-Communist League (WACL), founded in 1966, whose inspiration was General Chiang Kai-shek. The WACL was widely mocked for the bizarre right-wing figures, including Joseph Coors, a US brewing magnate, and Sun Myung Moon, the head of the Moonies sect, who found a home in its ranks. Between 1984 and 1986 the WACL was headed by a retired US major general, John Singlaub. Singlaub, who had fought in Vietnam and had been chief of staff of US forces in South Korea, was dismissed after he publicly criticized President Jimmy Carter's decision to withdraw US troops from Korea. Singlaub thus took his place as a worthy successor to General Curtis LeMay, who, at the end the Second World War, urged the government to make a quick start on the Third, which would offer a splendid opportunity to crush the Soviet Union, bleeding as it was from the loss of more than twenty million of its citizens killed in the struggle with the Nazis. Singlaub went on to aid the terrorist actions of the Nicaraguan Contras.

According to Bernardo Neri's book *El Último Supremo*, in a document dated 15 June 1988 the dictator instructed the president of the Central Bank of Paraguay, Dr César Romeo Acosta, to open an account for him, Account 130 as it became known, and deposit in it Cheque 88-WS-52048 drawn on the International Commercial Bank of China in the amount of US$1,550,000. That sum soon disappeared into thin air.

The WACL seemed to have got some value out of its connection with Stroessner, who was able to bring together military and civilian figures from Brazil, Argentina, Chile, Bolivia and Uruguay in Operation Cóndor, coordinating the fight against the left in the Southern Cone, the southernmost countries of South America.

In mid-1986 the dictator ordered the finance minister, General César

Barrientos, to open other accounts, which received cash at the rate of three guaranies per litre from sales of gas-oil fuel by Petropar, the state oil company. Highway tolls accruing to the Ministry of Public Works and Communications were also milked for cash, which at one point totalled 4,000 million guaranies.

Documents submitted to court by those investigating the Stroessner fortune after his removal from power, show that he took out 4,000 million guaranies (some US$3.2 million) between August 1986 and January 1989 for his intelligence services at the rate of US$70,000 a month.

In 1981 Helmut Kohl, the German Christian Democratic Chancellor, who ruled the Federal Republic between 1982 and 1998, was seeking ways to acquire secret funds for his party from donors. Paraguay, with its well-known German connection, was a place where donors, real or counterfeit, could be found.

The German weekly *Der Spiegel* reported in February 2000 that an unnamed businessman was given up to US$5,000 each for more than two hundred false death certificates sent to the German Christian Democratic Union (CDU); the doctor who issued them received US$200 for each. Part of the bargain was that in case of need the Paraguayan side would erect tombstones in Paraguayan cemeteries in the names given on the false death certificates.

The Hesse section of the CDU, which embraced German financial capital Frankfurt, said *Der Spiegel*, benefited from supposed legacies bequeathed to it by those whose alleged deaths were recorded on the false documents. The supposed bequests were passed through false accounts opened in a bank run by a Paraguayan businessman in the British Caribbean colony of Anguilla, a notorious centre for tax avoidance.

According to Paraguayan court documents the German CDU ruse was prepared by a group from Germany who went to Asunción in December 1981 on the occasion of an anti-communist conference in the Paraguayan capital under the auspices of the WACL, in which the government of Taiwan and the Argentine dictator General Roberto Viola would be involved. Negotiations were opened between the German group and the dictator, which yielded him tidy sums.

The visit also led to the establishment in September of the Institut für Deutsch–Paraguayische Beziehungen zur Wirtschafts und Kulturförderung (Institute for German–Paraguayan Economic Relations and Cultural Development) in Stuttgart, whose directors included very senior West German Christian Democrats, including two who were or had been ministers-president of German states, and senior Church figures. Those who joined the Institute paid a subscription of 50,000

Deutschmarks and received in return lots of government land. These lots were sold on to buyers in Paraguay for ten times the amount they had originally been valued at. The subscribers then passed on the profit to the CDU.

The details of the financial frauds that enriched the few and weakened the state were endless. Only a few were pursued by Paraguayan justice, and even fewer received their just deserts. After Stroessner's removal and the start of official investigations about corruption, for instance, a board member of the state telecommunications company, ANTELCO, and director of Radio Nacional, which kept up a barrage of threats and insults about Stroessner's enemies, was found to have US$11 million in an account at a Geneva branch of the Union des Banques Suisses. There was a further US$1.2 million in the Banco Exterior de España in Los Angeles, with more salted away in the British Caribbean colony of the Cayman Islands.

The state steel company Acepar provided a comfortable life for one general, who in 1989 was found to have swindled some US$4 million while his sister bought petrol, supposedly for the company, tax free, which she sold at the full price through the petrol pumps that she herself owned. They were forced to give back some US$3.3 million, somewhat less than what they owed the state.[12]

One of the most persuasive and personable of the group of financial sharks in the dictator's entourage was a media personality. Born in Argentina or Uruguay, he ingratiated himself with the dictator's inner circle, obtained Paraguayan citizenship and was named ambassador at large, operating from offices in Geneva, from where he committed a series of large frauds. One involved raising a credit of US$30 million from Italian suppliers for the construction of a factory to produce fruit juice in the town of La Colmena, which was never completed. After the fall of Stroessner, General Rodríguez threw him to the wolves. He was arrested in Miami, sent back to Paraguay and sentenced to seven years in jail. After completing part of the sentence he was extradited to face more charges in Switzerland.

One of Stroessner's ministers of health was more skilful at lining his own pockets than at improving the country's abysmal health standards. He became the owner of thirty-three estates, and through false documentation got himself regular access to ministry accounts fed by such as the Inter-American Development Bank with cash supposedly destined for the fight against malaria. Another account benefited from the ministry's

---

12. Neri (2003: 303).

false billing for the building of much-needed drains. The minister also benefited from regular payments by the ministry to 800 employees on its staff who did not exist. The price paid for a new National Hospital at Itauguá, one of the capital's suburbs, was US$95 million, of which about a third was stolen.

The sale of land around Itaipú also yielded cash for Stroessner's friends, who sold on acreages they had acquired cheaply to Brazilian farmers. Stroessner passed a law to promote rural settlements, whose execution was farmed out in 1963 to a new body, the Instituto de Bienestar Rural (IBR), the Rural Welfare Institute. Its aims were to 'transform the agrarian structure of the country through the effective incorporation of the peasant population into the social and economic development of the Nation through a just system of land distribution, technical and social assistance, adequate provision of credit, production and distribution to allow the rural producer his economic stability and a guarantee of his freedom and dignity and the basis of social welfare'. Being an invention of the Stroessner dictatorship, it was from the beginning tainted with corruption and futility. At the start of 2009, *ABC Color*[13] reflected the opinion of many when it commented:

> In the last sixty years of rule by the Colorados all the governments, principally that of the baleful dictatorship of Stroessner and his Institute of Rural Welfare [IBR], used natural resources as a slush fund to create a peasant clientele to sustain the Colorado Party, and as a business to sell to foreigners and locals at rock-bottom prices the world's best farm land and make multi-millionaires of a dozen agriculture ministers, presidents and directors of the IBR.

The reality was that the IBR officials in charge of land distribution sold the same piece of land to as many purchasers as they could and pocketed the proceeds with little or no regard for land titles. They also sold large extensions of land to big Brazilian companies, which split these up and sold them on to Brazilian farmers at a big mark-up. Even so, the Brazilians realized they could buy twice as much land in Paraguay as they could buy in their own country for the same amount.

Horacio Verbitsky, a distinguished Argentine journalist, author of *Robo por la Corona* and an expert in administrative corruption, explained some of the methods of corruption at Itaipú, Yacyretá and elsewhere in the government. Some public sector companies signed construction contracts with civil engineering firms which on purpose omitted a vital item from

---

13. *ABC Color*, 18 January 2009.

the agreement. When work was well advanced it was suddenly 'discovered' that the clause regulating vital work was missing and progress was halted while a new arrangement was made to cover the missing item. The state refused to pay extra and the case would go to law, with benefit to the lawyers involved. The case would be settled and the vital work completed, but the contractor would demand compensation for delay and the cost of contracting machinery for longer than expected. The cost overruns could reach very high figures, particularly if a badly paid government lawyer could be bribed to agree on its behalf to pay extensive compensation to the contractor. Everyone gained except the government.

The construction of the Yacyretá dam on the Paraná downstream from Itaipú was a promising new field for corruption for Paraguay and a neighbouring country. It began in 1983, when, as had been the case when Paraguay cooperated with Brazil, both Argentina and Paraguay were ruled by military dictatorships. It was inaugurated by President Juan Carlos Wasmosy and President Carlos Menem on 1 September 1994. As usual the projected cost of US$2.5 billion grew fast under the demands of the corrupt and by 2008 it exceeded US$15 billion. Like Itaipú it became a monument to outstanding civilian and electrical engineering and illustrated how the virus of corruption fostered by Stroessner lived on years after he was gone from the presidency. There was no money, however, for the victims of the dam whose houses had been flooded.

Carlos Menem, then president of Argentina, had long believed that the costs of the scheme would break all financial bounds. Talking to *ABC Color*, he pointed out that while the initial cost was estimated at US$1,500 million, with only half of the work completed that figure had risen to US$3,000 million, and he forecast 'if things continue like this it will cost US$12,000 million to complete it'.

According to its accounts on the last day of 2003, the unfinished Yacyretá had cost US$10,112 million, 40 per cent representing direct investments and 54 per cent the finance costs.

Domingo Poletti, the finance director of Itaipú, in an interview in Asunción in 1999, and uneasy perhaps about the questions relating to the scheme's production costs, said, 'Yacyretá has cost half what Itaipú costs and it produces about a quarter of the power that we do.' While the harnessing of the vast energy resources of the Paraná brought welcome transformation to Paraguay, it strengthened further the already strong position of the richest Paraguayans and made more difficult the task of constructing the more equitable society that Lugo wanted. It also bequeathed him the difficult task of obtaining a better price for the share of the electric power that Paraguay was selling to its neighbours.

LIBERATION THEOLOGY CALLED INTO QUESTION

As Lugo started his long process of transformation from churchman to politician, the fundamentals of liberation theology, so well set out in Vatican II and at the CELAM gatherings of Latin American bishops at Medellín and Puebla, were, as he knew, being sapped by many in the Church. They wanted to return to the days before Vatican II and hold back the changes promoted by John XXIII and what he called his *aggiornamento* or modernization. This was the scraping off from Church practices of accretions of tradition – from the use of fans of ostrich feathers to refresh popes during the most solemn ceremonies in St Peter's, the *flabellae*, to the continued use of Latin, a dead language, in much of the Church's ritual – which had little to do with the twentieth century. The anti-Vatican II forces tended to be socially conservative, indeed authoritarian, often aligning themselves with Spanish Francoists and clinging to the horror of democracy expressed by Pius IX in the nineteenth century. In the ranks of the opposition to Vatican II were people of many differing views. Some limited themselves to trying to revive the use of Latin; others – including a handful in Paraguay – followed their leader, Archbishop Marcel Lefebvre, into schism from Rome after his excommunication in 1988.

If there was one place where the deep historic roots of liberation theology came together to flower in modern times it was Peru. There a predominantly white minority lived in the style to which the former Spanish viceroys had become accustomed over the centuries following the Spanish conquest. The majority, the descendants of the great Andean civilizations whose astonishingly ambitious monuments were to be found everywhere from the desert city of Chan Chan to the mountain capitals of Cusco, Sacsahuamán and Machu Picchu, lived on the borders of hunger.

A leading liberation theologian was Gustavo Gutiérrez, born in Lima in 1928. He was ordained as a priest of that diocese and sent to various European universities. He devoted himself to the study of Bartolomé de las Casas. On his return to Peru, Gutiérrez was for a time in charge of the slum parish of Rímac in the Peruvian capital, but late in life he followed the example of Las Casas and entered the Dominican order.

Modern liberation theologians look back in particular to his book *La Teología de la Liberación* ('The Theology of Liberation'), which Gutiérrez published in 1951. The doctrine's flowering came at the 1968 bishops' gathering at Medellín, when they adopted a new consciousness of the 'inhuman misery in which the majority of the population lives' in their declaration. The meeting's final document said:

Indigence expresses itself as 'injustice which cries to the heavens'. But what perhaps has not been sufficiently said is that in general the efforts which have been made have not been capable of assuring that justice be honoured and realised in every sector of the respective national communities. Often families do not find concrete possibilities for the education of their children. The young demand their right to enter universities or centres of higher learning for both intellectual and technical training; the women, their right to a legitimate equality with men – the peasants, better conditions of life; or if they are workers, better prices and security in buying and selling; the growing middle class feels frustrated by the lack of expectations. There has begun an exodus of professional and technicians to more developed countries; the small businessmen and industrialists are pressed by greater interests and not a few large Latin American industrialists are gradually coming to be dependent on the international business enterprises. We cannot ignore the phenomenon of this almost universal frustration of legitimate aspirations which creates the climate of collective anguish in which we are already living.

'The poor', Gutiérrez said, 'have burst upon the social scene with "their poverty on their shoulders" – as Las Casas commented referring to the Indian nations of his time.'

There were, however, those who were not so keen on the example set by Las Casas, Vatican II and the Medellín conference, and who might be justifiably termed the Tortolo–Aramburu faction. Theirs had been a strong current of opinion in the Church. A strong statement, entitled 'Instruction on certain aspects of the "theology of liberation"', came from the Congregation for the Doctrine of the Faith (CDF), the former Holy Office presided over by the then Cardinal Joseph Ratzinger in 1984. The cardinal, concerned about left-wing influence on liberation theology, and going somewhat against the spirit of the final document from Medellín, said he wanted to

> draw the attention of pastors, theologians, and all the faithful to
> the deviations, and risks of deviation, damaging to the faith and to
> Christian living, that are brought about by certain forms of liberation
> theology which use, in an insufficiently critical manner, concepts
> borrowed from various currents of Marxist thought.

The strength of the conservative side in the Church which Lugo was to come up against was well illustrated by the case of Jon Sobrino, the Spanish-born Jesuit theologian at the Central American University in San Salvador. In November 2006 Sobrino received a public rebuke from the Vatican in the form of a '*notificatio*' from the CDF. Sobrino had narrowly escaped the US-trained army's murder squad at the university in 1989, who killed six of his fellow Jesuits, including Ignacio Ellacuría, like Sobrino a Basque and a distinguished liberation theologian, and two domestic staff.

The *notificatio* said that two of Sobrino's works, *La fe en Jesucristo* ('Faith in Jesus Christ'), published in 1999 and translated as *Christ the Liberator*, and *Jesucristo libertador: Lectura histórico-teológica de Jesús de Nazaret* ('Jesus Christ the Liberator: A historic and theological reading of Jesus of Nazareth'), published in 1991, 'contain propositions which are either erroneous or dangerous and may cause harm to the faithful'. It was not the worst sort of telling-off he could have received and there were no sanctions attached to it – he was not prevented from teaching, for instance – but it demonstrated that there were in the Church powerful people who were still very keen that liberation theology should not prosper.

On 13 December 2006, nearly two years after Lugo resigned from the diocese of San Pedro, Jon Sobrino wrote a powerful and emotional letter to his superior, Peter-Hans Kolvenbach, the Jesuit general. Its contents recounted the sort of treatment that liberation theologians were receiving from many in the Church hierarchy all over Latin America. Sobrino's reaction to this treatment was not just to reject the *notificatio* issued a month previously and to stand by his commitment to liberation theology, but also to hit back at those, including the pope, who had impugned his position.

On the question of the book published in 1991, Sobrino pointed out in his letter to Kolvenbach that its translation into Portuguese had been produced with the approval of Cardinal Paulo Evaristo Arns, at the time when he was archbishop of the Brazilian diocese of São Paulo, and had never before been questioned. The second one in 1999 had withstood the careful examination of a whole series of theological experts.

Sobrino described to his superior the sad story of thirty years of bad relations with senior figures in the Church, starting with Cardinal Garonne, at the time Prefect of the Congregation of Catholic Education, in 1975. 'The procedures of the Vatican were not always distinguished by their honesty and evangelical nature,' he commented. He went on to put his finger on one of the open sores of the Vatican in Latin America, the unwillingness of cardinals to allow the canonization of the murdered Archbishop Romero, who clearly died for his faith and would have been expected to be named a saint and a martyr. This unwillingness was to some extent linked to the archbishop's friendship with and reliance on Sobrino. Sobrino continued his letter with an account of his experience with Cardinal Alfonso López Trujillo, the Colombian arch-conservative member of the Vatican curia who was the fiercest opponent of liberation theology. After his appointment as cardinal in February 1983, López Trujillo left no doubt that he would 'finish with Gustavo Gutiérrez, Leonardo Boff, Ronaldo Muñoz and Jon Sobrino'. At a gathering of bishops in El Salvador in 1976 or 1977 to which, according to Sobrino, he had invited himself, López Trujillo had criticized Ellacuría and him. In a letter to Ellacuría the cardinal had denied it but, Sobrino told Kolvenbach, Arturo Rivera Damas, himself a bishop at the time and later archbishop of San Salvador, who was at the meeting, declared that he had indeed done so.

In Mexico in 1983 Cardinal Ernesto Corripio, the archbishop of Mexico City, forbade Sobrino to go ahead with a theological conference arranged by another religious order. In Honduras Archbishop Oscar Maradiaga of the capital, Tegucigalpa, scolded a group of nuns who had travelled from their home to the neighbouring diocese of Choluteca in order to hear a lecture by Sobrino which the local bishop, Raúl Corriveau, a French Canadian, had asked him to deliver.

In the late 1980s Sobrino was asked to talk to a group of laypeople in the Argentine Patagonia about their experiences under the military dictatorship at Viedma, the diocese of Bishop Hesayne. The bishop, who, with Kémérer, Angelelli and others, had done his best to protect local people from the terrorism of the military dictatorship, wrote to Sobrino telling him that the talk had been under discussion among the Argentine bishops with Cardinal Raúl Primatesta. Though the cardinal said he had never read any of Sobrino's books he opposed Sobrino's visit and thus the talk could not go ahead.

Sobrino later leant that Primatesta had told Hesayne that if Sobrino's talk did go ahead the pope, John Paul II, would not be visiting his diocese during his visit to Argentina.

In his letter, Sobrino gave his superior another reason why he would not accept the CDF's censure:

It has less to do directly with the Congregation of the Faith and more with the Vatican's way of proceeding in the last 20 or 30 years. In those years many theologians, men and women alike, good people – obviously with their limitations – with love of Jesus Christ and the Church and with great love for the poor have been persecuted mercilessly. And not just them. Bishops, too, as you know, Monsignor Romero when he was alive (there still are people in the Vatican who do not like him, at least they do not like the real Monsignor Romero but a watered-down Monsignor Romero), Dom Helder Câmara [originally a bishop in São Paulo later exiled to the north-eastern Brazilian archdiocese of Olinda and Recife], and Proaño, Don Samuel Ruiz [bishop of Las Casas's old diocese of San Cristóbal in Chiapas] and a long list of others. They have tried to behead, sometimes with black arts the Council of Latin American Religious and thousands of men and women religious of immense generosity which is all the more painful in the light of the humility of many of them. And on top of it all they have done their best to make the basic Christian communities, the little people, the privileged people of God, disappear.

Sobrino's letter continued with a detailed and critical theological examination of the reasons the CDF had given for its criticism of his work.

Another particularly dramatic case for the liberation theology that Lugo embraced and the storms that constantly seemed to surround it concerned the two Boff brothers, both Brazilian theologians well known to him. During the 1980s Clodovis Boff, a member of the ancient Servite order, lost his teaching post at the Pontifical Catholic University in Rio de Janeiro and was banned from teaching at the Marianum, the theological faculty of his order, in Rome. Still a Servite friar, Clodovis went to live in the Brazilian city of Curitiba and taught at its Pontifical Catholic University. He was never accused of doctrinal offences.

In an essay published in 2007 in the *Revista Eclesiástica Brasileira* (run by the Brazilian Franciscans and directed from 1972 until 1986 by his brother Leonardo), Clodovis Boff broke with liberation theology, or rather with 'the principal error' upon which, in his judgement, it was founded. He had hard words for his brother's ways of theological thought. He criticized what he saw as liberation theologians' excessive concentration on the poor. That, he said, could be disastrous for the Church. It would reduce the faith to mere politics and an instrument of social liberation, part of a popular movement competing with other political views and making the Church into a non-governmental organization. By failing to understand the current spiritual malaise, liberation theology, Clodovis argued, showed itself to be 'culturally myopic and historically anachronistic'.

For his part, Leonardo Boff, who was to be one of the guests at Lugo's inauguration in 2008, replied to his brother's essay. In an article published on the website of the Instituto Humanitas Unisinos on 27 May he remained absolutely firm in his commitment to liberation theology. He would not give up his view of the centrality of the poor in the Gospel. Framing the most powerful charge than one Christian theologian could aim at another, he added that to say anything else would be to 'place oneself outside the inheritance of Jesus and the Apostles'.

In 1985 Leonardo had been banned from teaching in any Catholic theological faculty by the Congregation for the Doctrine of the Faith, principally because of his book *Church, Charism and Power: Liberation Theology and the Institutional Church*. He left the Franciscan order, got married and went to live at Petrópolis, the former summer capital of the Brazilian emperors outside Rio.

In the Instituto Humanitas Unisinos article he hit back at his brother for his abandonment of liberation theology, saying, for instance, 'My suspicion is that the criticisms raised by Clodovis Boff to Liberation Theology will give to the church authorities in Brazil and Rome the weapons to condemn it once again and, who knows, banish it once and for all from the church.' Referring to the job of theologians to tend the flame of faith, he ended: 'Our mission is to feed it all the time because if it's hidden all that is sacred and worthy of the human being becomes a dead star and will mean a plunge into the abyss.'

Nevertheless, Leonardo Boff's pessimism was not shared by all. In June 2008 the new Jesuit general, Adolfo Nicolás, indicated clearly that, as far as he was concerned, there was much to be said for liberation theology, despite the fact that it was under threat. In an interview with the Barcelona newspaper *El Periódico*, Nicolás said liberation theology was 'a courageous and creative response to an unbearable situation of injustice in Latin America. As with any theology, it needs years to mature. It's a shame that it has not been given a vote of confidence and that soon its wings will be cut before it learns to fly. It needs more time.'

BISHOP OF POVERTY

In the midst of the fight over what should be the nature of liberation theology, Lugo, well schooled and with pastoral experience, was in March 1994 chosen to be bishop of one of the poorest places in Paraguay.

During his ten years as bishop of the indigent diocese of San Pedro Apóstol del Ycuamandeyú, Fernando Lugo had perforce to hone his political and administrative skills. He had experience of achieving the near-impossible. At the end of his time at San Pedro he was to say that he never felt himself worthy of the nomination, always worried about his capacity to do it justice and accepted it only at the urgent request of the nuncio of the day, José Sebastián Laboa.

Talking to journalists in San Pedro after the announcement of his resignation in January 2005, he said, 'When they named me I wanted to find a thousand reasons to decline or accept the responsibility ... This argument about not feeling myself worthy of the responsibility or having the capability I bore throughout these long years ... it kept me thinking all the time about whether I was doing things right for this diocese.' Despite his worries, in subsequent years Lugo became the foremost cleric to champion poor country people and indigenes and help them out of the morass into which thirty-six years of *stronismo* had plunged them.

In 2004, the year before he resigned from it, the *Annuario Pontificio* said his diocese contained 380,787 people of whom more than 90 per cent, or 350,000, were deemed to be Catholics. They were distributed in nineteen parishes looked after by ten diocesan or 'secular' priests and eight priests belonging to religious orders of various kinds. There were therefore 19,444 Catholics for each of the men capable of saying mass for the congregations and bringing them the sacraments. In addition there were nine lay brothers, and twenty nuns. In contrast to San Pedro, other parts of the Church seemed to be swimming in clerics. The diocese of Boston, Massachusetts, had only 1,361 inhabitants per priest. Moreover, the average income of its inhabitants was many times greater than the skimpy earnings of those in San Pedro.

As he settled into his new job the new bishop did as much as he could to encourage the Basic Church Communities (CEBs, *comunidades eclesiais de base*). These were made up of members of the Church who gathered together for prayer at the parish churches or elsewhere. The shortage of priests in a Latin American diocese like his had been a pre-occupation of Rome's for many decades but in the absence of ministers who could say mass, the central act of Catholic worship, alternatives had to be sought – though conservatives were worried that the CEBs would become the arrowhead of liberation theology and threaten the sense of hierarchy implicit in the system of bishops in their diocese and parish priests in their parishes.

The emphasis was removed from the model of the diocese divided up into parishes, each with a parish priest – or at least a share of a priest – who would be a focus of authority and guidance. Following the scheme well developed in Brazil, where there was a similar shortage of priests, the emphasis was transferred to the CEBs. In these, lay catechists chosen from among the people took on themselves the organization of the CEB life, conducting gatherings for prayers. These catechists did not have the facility of saying mass or administering the sacraments such as confession, but they did help to keep a communal religious life going. When Lugo arrived San Pedro had 650 CEBs; when he left there were twice as many. The CEBs were frowned on by conservatives, who stood aghast at the erosion of authority to which they were so committed.

It was not just the reorganization of the parishes which Lugo pushed forward. He decreed that the language of the Church in the diocese should be Guaraní, which was much better known and more widely used than Spanish. Nor did he choose to inhabit the bishop's residence, which he went to only on Fridays to attend to business matters. He lived in a small house indistinguishable from any other and went around the diocese on a motorbike. Nor did he go about in bishop's garb. According to Numa Molina, a Jesuit writing in *SIC*, the Venezuelan Jesuits' magazine, in August 2008, when he was asked whether it was a wrench to leave the bishopric, he replied, 'I didn't mind leaving since I hadn't been tied to the ring, the crosier and the privileges. I felt free: our first calling, as St Paul says, is to freedom.' By the time he arrived in his diocese General Rodríguez had been succeeded by yet another Colorado in elections held in conditions that would not have been un-familiar to Stroessner. The new head of state was Juan Carlos Wasmosy, a Colorado notable who had made his millions helping to build Itaipú. From 1975 to 1993 he headed Conempa, a consortium of Paraguayan and Brazilian companies which carried out the civil engineering work to their great profit. During his presidency Wasmosy retained his con-nection with Conempa, though he argued that it was now being run by his wife. A leader in the Asunción newspaper *La Nación* in January 1999 commented, 'The Wasmosy case is well known and no one can explain why he is not imprisoned and chained up in company with all his ministers and the congressmen on his payroll.'

If there was little hope for reform and change during Wasmosy's presidency, it was little better during that of his successor, Luis Ángel González Macchi. As the story of Stroessner and Lugo's uncle Epifanio had shown many years earlier, the Colorados had long been used to violent splits and bloody factionalism, and they constantly made their party into a nest of vipers. The most recent split went back to April 1996, when President Wasmosy sacked the army commander, General Lino César Oviedo, who had been the director of his presidential campaign in the 1993 elections. The ambitious Oviedo harboured bitterness that he himself had lost the contest with Wasmosy for the Colorado nomi-nation in those elections, and was desperate not to lose out a second time. The general refused to accept the president's order to go into retirement and, surrounded by senior officers loyal to him, persuaded

Wasmosy to accept a compromise by which he, Oviedo, would become defence minister with the undertaking that he would agree to resign from active service. At the last moment the president, worried by the storm of public protest that he was undermining civilian authority over the military by his concession to Oviedo, went back on his word and stopped his appointment to the ministry.

The events poured fuel on to the already fiercely burning fire of a Colorado rivalry between Oviedo's supporters, grouped into a faction called Unión Nacional de Colorados Éticos (UNACE), the National Union of Ethical Colorados, and another faction, the Movimiento de Reconciliación Colorada (MRC), Colorado Reconciliation Movement, led by a former foreign minister, Luis María Argaña, a bitter enemy of Wasmosy. Argaña accused Wasmosy of also cheating him out of the Colorado nomination in the primary election in December 1992.

On 27 October 1996, in a show of authority, Wasmosy ordered the arrest of Oviedo, who was sentenced to ten years' imprisonment for sedition for the events of 1996. Amid much plotting, Raúl Cubas Grau, a supporter of Oviedo, won the presidential elections of May 1998, beating his closest rival, the PRLA candidate Domingo Laíno, with a 54.5 per cent share of the vote. He took over from Wasmosy on 15 August with Argaña coming in as his vice-president. Two days after their installation Cubas freed Oviedo. This action produced a long sequence of political tensions which culminated in six days of bloodshed on the streets of the capital.

The killings started on 23 March 1999 with the assassination of Vice-President Argaña by his political enemies, who gunned him down in the back of the car taking him to his office and injured others in the car. As the news went around the capital a crowd of supporters of Argaña's MRC gathered in front of the hospital where the victims had been taken and demonstrated their anger with Cubas and those associated with Oviedo. The centre of the city filled with mainly young protesters carrying banners and placards with slogans such as 'Dictatorship never again'.

Oviedo's UNACE members retaliated, and when the bloodshed stopped on 29 March 769 people lay wounded, of whom seven died. The events became known as the Marzo Paraguayo, the Paraguayan March, and the reputation of Paraguayan politicians at home and abroad fell even farther than previously. At the same time Lugo's horrified reaction to these events, repeated in many public speeches, lifted his popularity.

The fighting eventually finished and Oviedo fled to Argentina in a light plane from a landing ground in the Chaco an hour or so before Cubas resigned the presidency and fled to the safety of the Brazilian embassy and the Brazilian air force plane that spirited him away to Brazil, where eventually he was given political asylum. Two days later the Public Prosecutor reported that $700,000 had been transferred from the governnment's Banco Nacional de Fomento to a presidential account some forty-eight hours before Cubas's resignation and flight. A decade after the overthrow of Alfredo Stroessner violence and peculation were still the main dishes on the country's political menu.

Oviedo was arrested in June 2000 in Brazil and held pending a request for his extradition from the Paraguayan authorities which never came. He voluntarily returned to Paraguay in February 2002, presented himself to the courts and was detained for his part in the killings of March 1999.

The election of Nicanor Duarte Frutos, a man who had been Wasmosy's minister for education and culture, raised hopes for better things not just in Paraguay but also in the wider world. That hope even tempted the president of Cuba to make an appearance at his inauguration in August 2003. Fidel Castro, never previously known for wasting his time with political leaders in whom he had no hope, was one of nine Latin American heads of state at the ceremony.

In San Pedro Lugo certainly prayed for the causes that he had adopted, but he backed up prayer with a succession of public pronouncements urging the government to do more for the poorest while at the same time encouraging the peasants to stand up for their rights.

He had no difficulty in saying that the Colorado governments were both irresponsible and incompetent. The establishment of a pro-government vigilante squad, the Commission for Citizens' Security, dedicated to imposing obedience on Asunción in San Pedro, was followed by evidence that they had had a hand in the murder of seven victims, one of whom was a child, five cases of torture, three wrongful imprisonments and dozens of cases of threats of violence. Lugo was to call them 'armed criminals' and 'terrorists'.[14]

More and more the bishop came to be seen as an unofficial leader of the opposition, and his support was quietly sought by a number of political groups. Several, including leaders of the Colorado party itself, sounded Lugo out on becoming a presidential candidate committed to the campaign against poverty and unemployment. As rumours circulated,

14. Centro de Investigación de Relaciones Internacionales y Desarrollo, Barcelona, www.cidob.org/es/documentación.

he himself came out with his own strong statement in September 2001: 'To be with the people and fulfil my mission is much more attractive and comforting for me. The ups and downs of a political life don't attract me in the least.'

Nevertheless, three months later he called for a popular mobilization against the government of González Macchi (who had come to power in March 1999), which, he said, was incapable of offering solutions 'to the great problems of the country such as dishonesty, impunity from the law, poverty, lack of education, and reactivation of the economy, above all in the countryside'.

The government of Luis González Macchi was certainly presiding over chaos, and a mass of evidence of corruption and incompetence came to the surface. In May 2001 the president's name appeared on the list of people the Fiscal General, or State Prosecutor, was investigating over the case of US$16 million which had gone missing after the winding up of two banks. The cash was discovered in a branch of Citibank in New York in the account of a humanitarian foundation which was on the point of making a gift of half that sum to a consultancy firm owned by the president's sister, Judith González Macchi. Those alleged to be implicated in the operation were a brother of the president, a judge; the president's father; and his father's brother, who was obliged to resign from the board of the Council against Corruption.

On further investigation evidence emerged that one of the cars in the president's fleet, a large BMW, had been reported stolen in Brazil and brought secretly across the border. The presidential team was involved not just in contraband but in counterfeiting of consumer products. In April 2002 the State Prosecutor formally charged González Macchi with regard to the missing US$16 million. The next month the Auditor General accused him of offences relating to the privatization of Copaco, the Compañía Paraguaya de Telecomunicaciones. The company was sold for US$200 million when a previous valuation had put its worth at $400 million. Such financial manoeuvres connected to privatizations had become common under dictatorships in Latin America after General Augusto Pinochet used them widely for the enrichment of himself and his family in the 1970s.[15]

Lugo's repeated calls for people to go into the streets to protest against 'bad politicians' brought relations between the government and the bishops to a point of acute tension. This was well expressed by the incoming Colorado president, Nicanor Duarte, who in May 2003

---

15. O'Shaughnessy (2000: 144ff).

loosed off a broadside against 'the hypocrites and false teachers' who were building their nests in the Catholic Church.

Lugo had to tread a difficult path in his diocese, urging the poor to claim their rights and press for a fairer system of landownership and an end to Colorado corruption while at the same time trying to persuade them to abstain from violence. He spoke against the idea of Paraguay joining the Free Trade Area of the Americas, FTAA, which would have opened the country's frontiers to a flood of US produce subsidized by the government in Washington, undercutting the livelihoods of Paraguayan farmers, as was increasingly happening to the farmers of Mexico as cheap maize flowed over their country's northern border.

At the same time, in June 2000 he joined a large number of peasants – estimated at between 3,500 and 8,000 – from the town of San Pedro and surrounding villages who gathered for three days to demand that the government undertake to surface the main trunk road, Route III, immediately. It was one of the actions that made him a hero to the poor in San Pedro.

Politics, international and national, continued to fascinate the bishop of San Pedro. Talking to the Buenos Aires daily *Página 12* on 30 January 2009, Lugo recalled how he had taken time off from his diocese to attend the first meeting of the World Social Forum in Porto Alegre, the southern Brazilian metropolis, in 2001. The gathering had been convened in the humbler surroundings of a Brazilian city to do for supporters of social change what the World Economic Forum was doing for the supporters of conservatism in the expensive Swiss Alpine resort of Davos.

At the same time Lugo spoke out strongly against the climate of violence and insecurity that was overtaking the countryside, where landowners sought in every conceivable way to hang on to the land that many of them had acquired by illegal means. A habit of kidnapping came into vogue, which claimed as one of its victims Cecilia, the daughter of former president Cubas, who was found murdered soon after her kidnapping in February 2005.

Indefatigably Lugo pressed for more money from central government for one of the poorest departments. In landowning circles he was known, *inter alia*, as 'the bishop of the left' and 'the guerrilla bishop'. Yet the strain of keeping to a careful line of condemning the government while he restrained its opponents was a difficult one for him to follow.

GOODBYE TO SAN PEDRO

On 7 January 2005, without consulting the majority of the bishops, Lugo announced that he was resigning as bishop of San Pedro. He had in fact sought Rome's permission to lay down his responsibilities in a letter delivered to John Paul II on 17 April 2004, in which he had argued health reasons for his request. Commenting on his decision shortly after the announcement, he confessed darkly to a feeling of impotence that his job as a bishop brought him,

> ... the impotence of not being able to see the institutional way forward, and of not being able to help so many families who had their human rights humiliated, because of the young people who want to study and work and can't because of a lack of money and, on the other hand, observe impotently that the institutions of the state did not have the capacity of giving answers to the needs of this population that I as a pastor would have liked to have given more dignity.[16]

At the same time he added, 'I love the diocese, I've got a great affection for the clergy, for the church and for the task I have as a pastor and nothing prompts me to say, "I'm leaving this and going to devote myself to something else."' He added to the *ABC* reporter in San Pedro, 'There exist many temptations, among which the idea of party politics does not figure. That doesn't attract me. I'll continue to be a priest.'

Though he had left his diocese his spirit lived on in San Pedro, where a few days after his departure prominent figures there brought out a statement calling the Duarte government 'unconstitutional, anti-democratic and unchristian'. 'No one has licence to imprison, beat up or kill citizens,' the notables said, giving the impression that, in San Pedro at least, the worst days of Stroessner's terror had returned.

The different reactions to the announcement of Lugo's departure, which took most Paraguayans by surprise, crystallized the attitudes that various sectors of society adopted towards him. As a man in episcopal orders he maintained his personal position and was given the title of 'bishop emeritus', one given to a number of men whose position in the Church was out of the ordinary.

The mayor of San Pedro called a press conference, and in a tone of the deepest sorrow cried out in Guaraní, '*Mba'ere ore reja?*' – 'why are you leaving us?' He said that Lugo's departure was a great loss for the whole community. 'Those on the margins of society are without their only support,' he added.

The president of the governing council of the department of San Pedro, a Colorado, Arnaldo Ruiz Díaz, said his departure was a shame, he had done much for the department and his presence had been very

---

16. *ABC Color*, 11 January 2005, quoted in Andrada Nogués (2008: 32).

positive. Another member of the departmental council, Clara de Zimmermann, said, 'In a society where there are so many disappointments and lack of trust in the authorities, Monsignor Lugo was the repository of the people's trust and hope.'

ABC's correspondent in San Juan Bautista, the diocese of the sixty-nine-year-old Mario Melanio Medina, took the opportunity of Lugo's departure to tilt at the pusillanimous nature of most of the hierarchy.

> The departure of the bishop of San Pedro reveals the human weakness, the lack of firmness, of civic and patriotic courage of many of Paraguay's bishops who instead of dotting the 'i's and backing their colleagues against the powerful have shrunk back to their churches. Lugo and Medina are the only ones who used to confront the unjust, corrupt and venal people who sit astride government.

For his part Dr Enrique Riera Figueredo, a former president of the Asociación Rural del Paraguay, the landowners' organization, called him a 'revolutionary politician' who always 'supported land invasions and the blocking of highways'. Talking to *ABC Color*, Riera said, 'I used to say to him: if you support the occupations, why don't you take off your cassock and go with your peasants with a rifle on your shoulder?'

For their part the bishops' reactions were ones of confusion. Claudio Giménez, bishop of Caacupé, said he knew nothing of the letter written by Lugo to the pope in April which Giménez said was personal and whose contents were revealed only in January 2005. Ignacio Gogorza, bishop of Encarnación, reminded his listeners that Lugo had been firmly on the side of liberation theology but added, 'It hasn't got the strength it once had in the 1970s.'

Lugo made his way back to Encarnación, where he had grown up, and took over the parish of San Roque González de Santa Cruz while the parish priest went on holiday. Talking to a reporter on the Asunción newspaper *La Nación* in May he said, 'I had my sixth attack of thrombosis in my left leg and that's why I came to Encarnación where I feel at ease.' (He had indeed sought treatment for the thrombosis from doctors in Brazil quite often.) The rhythm of life in his former diocese, he said, 'is slower in the north and here there's more business activity, investments, development and capital flows which mean that people live more comfortably'. He added that there was a lack of land, demanding a real agrarian reform that the government was not promoting. His stay in the parish allowed him to get up to date with the situation of those suffering from the rise in water levels behind the Yacyretá dam. After his resignation the title of bishop emeritus was a useful one to have as he was more and more drawn into political work. The latter was not seen by some bishops to be seemly. The criticisms grew after the events of March 2006.

By February 2006 he was back in San Pedro, attending a meeting at the village of Yrybukua, where he seized another opportunity to criticize the government, calling President Nicanor Duarte and his interior minister, Rogelio Benítez, 'terrorists'. He said the authorities themselves were responsible for the prevailing sense of fear and insecurity and criticized their silence over the acts of violence committed by the vigilantes of the Guardias Ciudadanas or Civilian Guards. 'How different it would have been if they had killed one of Nicanor's sons,' he declared.

The landowners, meanwhile, did not sit idly by as the peasants made their demands. By May 2006 peasant leaders were claiming that 13,000 members had been inducted into the Civilian Guards, trained and given access to weapons. In Lugo's region of San Pedro, where the growing of soya was expanding, they had caused the deaths of ten peasants.

At the same time Lugo's personal situation was being overshadowed by the great political affair of the day. Duarte wanted to exercise the leadership of the Colorados without having to lay down the presidency, a situation that would have given him enormously more power and was against the spirit and by any unbiased judgement against the letter of the constitution. Despite this, on 8 March the Supreme Court of Justice gave the verdict to the president with a favourable vote of five members of the court. Two days later, in a joint declaration, the bishops condemned the verdict as opening the way to another round of authoritarianism and said that they shared the 'worry and indignation' that the Supreme Court's decision had provoked. The stage was set for the battle over the future of legitimate democracy in a Paraguay that had not had great experience of it. It was to stir the Paraguayans, laying the basis of a political battle that Lugo would win nearly two years later.

A NUNCIO CALLS

At this crucial moment in Paraguayan politics the Vatican decided to change its representative in Asunción. The new nuncio, Orlando Antonini, sixty-two, arrived on 19 March 2006 just as Asunción was on the point of political combustion. He looked tired after his long flight and was doubtless exercised by the challenges he would clearly be facing within days of his arrival thanks to the actions of the former bishop of San Pedro. He presented his letters of credence to President Duarte on 24 March as the final preparations for Lugo to head the demonstration against the government on Wednesday, 29 March were being made. He was in time to be active and in a front seat for the impending events, which changed the life of Lugo, and indeed of Paraguay, and to be in a key position at the climax of Lugo's time as a bishop. Tens of thousands of Paraguayans, who normally never pondered legal matters from one year's end to the other, felt deeply about Duarte's attempt at constitutional trickery and were eager for a leader who would help them towards a just solution.

The crowds that poured into the streets of the capital surprised the police, who had planned for some 10,000 people. The government had got wind of the ambition of the organizers of the demonstration and had put about the rumour that Lugo himself was in grave danger of harm from the hands of extremists. This falsehood, if it were widely believed, could have allowed Duarte to ban it. In the event it was the largest demonstration since the overthrow of Stroessner in 1989. Some 35,000 in fact appeared, in a massive act of repudiation of the government and the judges.

The organizers called themselves Citizens' Resistance and the event was called '¡Kueraima Paraguay!' ('Paraguay has had enough!' in Guaraní). They came from a hundred different organizations, the PLRA (the Authentic Radical Liberal Party), the Patria Querida, Oviedo's UNACE and many more, with the supporters of each jostling hard to be seen to be as close as possible to Lugo. Schoolchildren and students mocked the president, with one imaginative young man dressing himself up as Louis XIV of France. All joined in the national anthem. The principal speaker and acknowledged and undisputed inspirer of the event was Lugo. He was wearing a bullet-proof vest. The crowds behaved themselves impeccably.

The job of a nuncio as representative of the Sovereign Pontiff is often a difficult one and, though making him powerful in countries where Catholics are influential and active, is little understood. He has two roles; one is to represent the policies of the Vatican to the government he is accredited to, suggesting perhaps how its representative should vote in the United Nations on an issue in which the Holy See has an interest. His second is influencing the religious life of the country in which he is stationed and reporting back on it to Rome. Given that by the twentieth century the Vatican had succeeded in monopolizing the appointment of bishops round the world, the job included suggesting to the papacy that Father X would be likely to make a better bishop than Father Y, who might be developing a drink problem, in the diocese of Z, which, the nuncio would diplomatically point out, needed a new one quickly. After all, it had been without a pastor since the last one retired three years previously after that regrettable situation with his housekeeper and those wretched lottery tickets.

In some Catholic countries the nuncio is the dean of the diplomatic corps, the most senior foreign diplomat, ex officio from the moment of his arrival. Living in one of the grandest houses in any capital, flying the gold-and-white colours of the Holy See from his flagpole, a nuncio is likely to appear in the social columns of those newspapers that have such a thing. These are likely to be conservative ones. It is not to be wondered at that he seems to be more the grand representative of the Sovereign Pontiff than a humble labourer in the Lord's vineyard devoted to proclaiming the simple messages of the Babe of Bethlehem. Yet at the same time a nuncio can be the target of attacks from all sides – the government, the local bishops and priests, the laity and on occasion Rome if he is seen as having 'gone native' and become too aligned with the locals. Sometimes, if he is particularly arrogant and clumsy (as in the case of Pio Laghi, born in 1922, the baleful General Videla's tennis partner in Buenos Aires who offered no defence of those who were the object of atrocities at the hands of the military and was a source of shame for the Catholic Church), the criticisms of him are justified.

Antonini's mentor had for long been Carlo Martini, who has been credited with persuading him to seek a post in the Vatican diplomatic service, a large majority of whose members are Italian. Martini was appointed nuncio to Paraguay in 1958 at the beginning of the Stroessner dictatorship and made archbishop three years later. From the beginning of his stay in Paraguay, Martini had faced difficult circumstances. He went on to be nuncio in Mexico in 1970, always a headache for the Church.

Antonini started off in the nunciatures in Bangladesh, a Muslim state; Madagascar, the former French colony; Syria, again Muslim with a strong presence of Catholics of the oriental rite, always jealous of too much supervision from Rome; Chile, when the country was recovering from the bloodbath of the Pinochet dictatorship; the Netherlands; and then France. He also served time in head office in charge of the Vatican's relations with Central America, where, over half a century, hundreds of thousands of innocents had been massacred. Guatemala bore the scars of the Washington-backed invasion, the right wing *coup d'état* of 1954 and a subsequent genocide; Nicaragua was still reeling from the attacks it had suffered from the US-supported Contra terrorists during the Reagan presidency; and El Salvador remained in the power of the US-trained military. They had shot Archbishop Oscar Romero, archbishop of San Salvador, in 1980, the six Jesuits and two domestic staff on the campus of their Central American University on 16 November 1989, and four US churchwomen eight months later.

Romero's murder was a source of division at the Vatican, with some saying that he was clearly a martyr who should be canonized without delay and the conservatives pointing to his partiality for liberation theology and seeking to block any progress on canonization.

In 1998, having helped to plan the tricky but ultimately successful papal visit to Cuba, Antonini accompanied John Paul II to Havana and helped the pope in his talks with Fidel Castro and other senior Cuban leaders.

In 1999, already tested by fire, Antonini was named nuncio to Zambia and Malawi, where he was to remain until 2005. In Lusaka, the Zambian capital, he had to deal with the unique and bizarre case of Emmanuel Milingo, the capital's archbishop, who had resigned his see in 1983 and had gone on to marry a Korean bride in a Moonie ceremony, before trying and failing to achieve a reconciliation with Rome. Milingo was excommunicated in September 2006.

The Italian-born Antonini was ordained a priest in 1968, just as the Church was digesting the reforms of Vatican II. He got his doctorate in canon law and in 1980 went into the Vatican diplomatic service. He was to play an important part in the developing impasse between Lugo and his superiors in Rome.

Not only does a nuncio have to navigate among the various rocks and shoals of Church and government politics in the country or countries to which he is accredited. He also has to keep close to the course of the (usually quiet) political blizzards that constantly sweep through the Holy See, the government of the Church which claims the loyalty of a billion Catholics and their bishops and priests in almost every country, and whose decisions have worldwide importance. The Holy See is presided over by the successor of St Peter, the Sovereign Pontiff, in the Vatican City. The Stato della Città del Vaticano consists of 44 hectares with a few outlying specks of land in and around Rome, a rather smaller area than that of the US embassy in Baghdad. It was brought into existence in 1929 under an agreement between the papacy and the Italian government and gives the popes a tiny territorial area over which they are sovereign, enabling them to join international bodies of other sovereign states. It replaces the Papal States, which used to embrace much of central Italy and were done away with in the late nineteenth century. Papal armies are a thing of the past but there remains a richly uniformed Swiss Guard, German-speaking Swiss with military experience. The popemobiles bear the registration plate SCV1 (a situation that gives rise to the old legends that VAT 69 is the popes' whisky of choice or possibly their telephone number).

The Holy See is not a democracy and the pope answers to no one on earth. In a carefully gradated hierarchy his principal assistants in his curia or court are the cardinals. They are often pompously called 'the princes of the Church': Joseph Hurley, an outspoken US churchman who became a papal diplomat, in 1940 the bishop of a diocese in Florida and later an archbishop, called them 'old men in dresses'. Those of them under eighty have the job of electing a new pope on the death of the old one. At the end of 2008 there were 192 cardinals, the largest group by nationality being Italian.

Benedict XVI's nineteenth-century predecessor Pius IX formally declared papal infallibility at the First Vatican Council in 1870 – against the wishes of some of the bishops present. The proclamation, extended to some degree to the bishops of the Church, was repeated at Vatican II. Never did the papacy claim that it would never make mistakes or that popes would never commit offences. It merely confirmed the belief long held in the Church that whatever a pope proclaimed on matters of faith and morals to the whole Church was inspired by the Holy Spirit and therefore true. The pope and his tiny staff in the curia often witness the most bitter of international and ecclesiastical rivalries, many going back centuries.

It was much to the credit of the subtle Antonini that the impasse over Lugo's awkward position in the Church was somewhat eased. Six months after the news of Lugo's departure from San Pedro the chances of such a resolution seemed slim. In June 2006, some weeks after the appearance of Lugo at the mass demonstration of 29 March, a very senior figure in the Vatican, Cardinal Franc Rodé, the Slovenian prefect of the Congregation for Institutes of Consecrated Life and Societies of Apostolic Life, the Vatican's watchdog over the activities of the religious orders, arrived in the Paraguayan capital. He was to preside over one of the periodical meetings of the Conference of Clergy of Latin America and the Caribbean which Sobrino had said the conservatives were seeking to rein in. A former archbishop of Ljubljana, he was no enthusiast for any weakening of the position of the clergy in the Church. In relation to the weakening of the Church in France and Quebec, where many clergy has sought laicization, he announced, 'Today we see the emergence of a generation of politicians or cultural leaders who are completely ignorant of the Christian tradition.' He did not want to have any part in losing a bishop.

As he arrived at the airport, Rodé was asked about the idea that Lugo should stand for the presidency. He was categorically against such an idea. 'It is not the task of a bishop to be involved in a political candidacy. That mission corresponds to the laity,' he said. He added that in the years following Vatican II experience had shown that politics and ideology were not the best fields for the Church or the clergy. Nevertheless, he left open a window of opportunity, saying that if Lugo discovered that that was his new mission he should go to the Vatican and seek the permission of the Holy See.

As the year progressed the tension built up as Lugo was more and more seen as the only candidate with enough clout to ensure the end of more than sixty uninterrupted years of Colorado rule.

Nevertheless, he went on sitting on the fence and announcing his unwillingness to quit the priesthood while his friends were hard at work preparing the ground – and the Paraguayans – for the day when he would declare himself. The day after the demonstration he was saying that he was 'not a politician in the literal sense of that word ... I'll simply be a social actor and a citizen and I think that's the most that moves me'.

THE CANDIDACY

In May 2006 Lugo was saying the same, replying 'No, no, no, no' to a question about whether he was going to seek the presidency in the 2008 elections. Nevertheless, expectations rose. At the end of November several hundred people gathered at the Divine Word College in the capital, where they called on Lugo to accept the petition they had prepared for him to seek the presidency. On 17 December the Movimiento Popular Tekojoja (the Tekojoja Popular Movement), a group committed to securing the presidency for Lugo, was presented to the public by the organizers at a meeting that attracted more than 1,500 people. The backgrounds of the organizers gave a flavour of Tekejoja's political stance – José Parra, a peasant leader from San Pedro, and Agripino Silva had both stood for the Senate in 2003 on the platform of the Patria Libre (Free Fatherland) Party, a nationalist party of the left; Ramón Riquelme, a singer with the Los Corales group, was also from Patria Libre; Guillermina Kanonikov (who had, as we have seen, been close to the OPM and had chaired the recent meeting at the Divine Word College the previous month); Miguel Ángel López, a teacher also formerly of the OPM; Dr Aníbal Carrillo Iramáin, a paediatrician and a member of a medical union with a record of resistance against Stroessner; and Sixto Pereira, a peasant leader from the Cordillera department.

The group invited all Paraguayan men and women, resident foreigners, Christian men and women and non-believers to join the movement,

10 Lugo announces his intention of seeking the presidency, Encarnación, Christmas Day, 2006.

and hundreds marched off to the Divine Word College. There Lugo made his first public speech announcing his intention to stand for the presidency. Tekejoja and the friends it contained gave him a good start. It was, however, not the organization which was to bring him to the presidency. It was too unruly and did not have the political skills the candidacy needed.

His formal announcement of his decision to stand for the presidency came in a letter to the pope dated 18 December 2006 and delivered to the nunciature on 21 December. If Lugo let off an artillery round towards Rome from Asunción, Rome had one ready for firing at the same time. Cardinal Giovanni Battista Re, prefect of the Congregation of Bishops and simultaneously president of the Pontifical Commission for Latin America, and the Congregation's secretary, Archbishop Francesco Monterisi, wrote to him on 20 December with a solemn admonition about his conduct vis-à-vis his desire to stand for the presidency.

Five days later, on Christmas Day 2006, at the age of fifty-five, Lugo made his long-expected public announcement of his decision to stand for the presidency in the doorway of the house in Encarnación in which he had spent decades of his life, an unprepossessing brick structure with a rather shabby wooden porch over a front door painted green.

'Those who know my family,' he said, 'and those who know me well know that I discriminated against no one and that, at the same time, many who have seen me as a boy selling coffee and pasties around the city know I haven't changed.'[17]

With a rhetorical flourish he added, 'I swear before the heroes and martyrs of the Fatherland that I will stay faithful to the principles that with so much courage those martyrs and heroes upheld. I swear before God and the Fatherland that I will shape my conduct rigorously to the values which expressly seek the common good. If I do not, let God, the Fatherland and history be my judges!'

With that he boarded a van and started a tour round the city, thus starting a presidential campaign that did not end until 20 April 2008.

As one might have expected, the Paraguayan bishops' conference did its best to side with Benedict without being hostile to Lugo. Individual bishops took a harder line. Rogelio Livieres Plano, bishop of Alto Paraná and a member of the conservative Opus Dei movement, which was founded in the Spain of General Franco and had never been able to rid itself of a reputation for secrecy, said that Lugo's action was a 'dagger pointed at the Church'. Interviewed by Hugo Ruiz Olazar of *ABC Color*,[18] he said:

> There is something bad for catholic doctrine and canon law that a bishop quits his ministry and devotes himself to some other task, even one as noble as that of politics. We're sorry that the means that we use to improve the world, the preaching of the word of God and the sacraments are insufficient in the eyes of a bishop to do good to society and he chooses earthly means. That's to undervalue the supernatural means that the Church has used for the past 2,000 years. For the past hundred years that's been forbidden to us. Earlier members of the clergy used to take part in revolutionary councils. The Pope himself was king of half Italy. It was progress when the Church moved away from political activity and returned to its origins.

In a newspaper interview published on the last day of 2006, Lugo described his political views to a reporter: 'I believe in equality, in equity,

---

17. *ABC Color*, 26 December 2006.
18. Ibid., 31 July 2008.

in an independent and autonomous system of justice, in a state that doesn't organise every matter in the Republic, but neither in a state that is absent. There are no pure ideologies today. I believe that all the ideologies have helped us.'

He went on to coin a phrase about his political stance for which he became famous: '*Mbytetépe, poncho jurúica*' ('In the centre, like the hole in a poncho'). During the election campaign, too, Lugo looked back to his days in uniform in Encarnación and reminded voters that the sort of knowledge he had acquired in earlier years of military discipline on how to handle a rifle, a machine gun and explosives was invaluable for someone who sought the presidency and with it the supreme command of Paraguay's armed forces.

The low point in relations between Lugo and the Vatican came as a swift riposte to the news that the bishop had finally made public his decision to stand for the presidency. Issued at the Vatican on 20 January 2007, barely three weeks after Lugo's announcement, the few words of the decree dripped such icy disdain and anger that they deserve to be quoted *in extenso*.

SUSPENSION A DIVINIS OF H.E.
MGR FERNANDO LUGO MÉNDEZ, S.V.D.
BISHOP EMERITUS OF SAN PEDRO

DECREE

On 21 December 2006 the Apostolic Nuncio in Paraguay delivered to you the text of a Canonical Warning inviting you not to accept the candidacy to the Presidency of Paraguay, making you aware that if you did ... there would be imposed on you – as a first step – the canonical penalty of suspension which prohibits sacred ministers from all acts pertaining to order and jurisdiction (can. 1333 § 1).

Considering that on 25 December 2006, the feast of the Lord's Nativity, Your Excellency declared publicly your willingness to accept political or institutional responsibilities and so far you have not changed your decision, with sincere pain I carry out my duty of imposing on Your Excellency the present Decree, the penalty of suspension a divinis in line with canon 1333 § 1 prohibiting you from exercising the power of order and government and the exercise of all functions and rights inherent in the office of bishop.

With this penal sanction you remain in the clerical state and continue to be bound to the duties inherent in it, though suspended from the sacred ministry.

I trust that Your Excellency will reiterate your decision to be faithful to the obligations you freely assumed when you were consecrated bishop.

Given in the Vatican City in the seat of the Congregation for Bishops, 20 January 2007.

Giovanni Battista Card. Re (Prefect)
Francesco Monterisi (Secretary)

As the newly proclaimed presidential candidate went into battle for the votes of the electorate, it was made clear to him by the Vatican that he would be fighting a parallel battle with the Church authorities. If he lost the second battle his defeat could mean his losing the first. The Colorados at first made it clear that they would do their best to impose the terms of the constitution, which specifically forbade a cleric from occupying the presidency.

They seemed to have Lugo caught in a constitutional armlock. The constitution seemed to prevent a cleric like him becoming president while the papacy was not allowing him to lay aside his clerical state. But Sixto Pereira, the man who had been in on the foundation of Tekejoja and was now second vice-president of the Senate, was at hand.

'There are signs', he announced coolly, 'that the main roads in all the departments of the country will be cut,' and he added that Lugo's candidature would bring about change in Paraguay. At the same time Juan Torales, the general secretary of the trade union federation, the Central Nacional de Trabajadores, warned that any move to block Lugo's candidacy would be the source of great popular frustration. 'It would result in a national mobilization,' he threatened.[19]

At the same time Lugo's lawyers weighed in and drew strength from Cardinal Re's very *suspensio a divinis*. They argued that the constitution laid down merely that a cleric should resign from the clergy and not exercise his functions. A rule of the Catholic Church could in no way impede a Paraguayan citizen in the exercising of his constitutional rights. Indeed, the Church itself had prevented him from exercising his episcopal functions. 'He has stopped being a minister of the Catholic religion,' they pointed out.

In April 2007 Lugo went to Havana with his closest friend and chief supporter among the bishops, Mario Melanio Medina of San Juan Bautista, for the Sixth Hemispheric Gathering of Struggle against

---

19. *ABC Color*, 31 January 2008.

11 Lugo with Federico Franco (left) after submitting election papers, 31 January 2008.

the Free Trade Treaties, which brought together some seven hundred delegates, including indigenous leaders, trade unionists, slum dwellers, clergy, campaigners for peace and many others united against US and European efforts towards free trade.

In an interview with *Juventud Rebelde*, the Havana newspaper, he said that if he won the presidency he would start a 'true, authentic and genuine process of change that the country wants'.

The immense popularity of Lugo in Paraguay did much to ensure his eventual victory in the 2008 elections. At the same time it could be argued that the division of the Colorados was at least as important.

In June 2007 the PLRA decided they would not put up their own candidate for the presidency on the understanding that they would support Lugo's in exchange for one of their members becoming his vice-presidential candidate.

In September the last piece of electoral masonry was put in place with the formation of the Alianza Patriótica para el Cambio, the Patriotic Alliance for Change, a dozen parties, all of them small with the exception of the PLRA.

As the date for polling approached Lugo's opponents tried to throw mud at him. The anonymous whispered accusations were that he was

involved in the kidnap and assassination of Cecilia, the daughter of
Raúl Cubas, the man who had been president for a few months from
15 August 1998; that he had a relationship with a woman which produced
a child; and that he was an active member of the Colombian guerrilla
organization FARC. Opinion polls showed that these campaigns had
the opposite effect to that which his opponents sought.

The organization that took advantage of the chaos in the Colorado
rank and file and did bring victory was the Alianza Patriótica para el
Cambio. It wedded a leader without a national party – Lugo – to a party
without national leaders – notably the Liberals. The APC harnessed his
personal popularity to the stable electoral rock of the PLRA. Despite
continuous internal squabbling, a series of mediocre leaders and the
dirty tricks of the Colorados, the principal Liberal faction had for nearly
two decades collected around a quarter of the popular vote.

Lugo's popularity brought out the votes for his presidential candidacy
and mobilized the country against the divided and discredited Colorados.
At the same time the PLRA, which had no presidential candidate who
came within a mile of rivalling Lugo's popularity, brought in the loyalties
of traditional Liberal voters and the machinery that gave Lugo strength
he would not otherwise have had in the Congress and among the aspir-
ants for the important governorships in the seventeen departments.

Lugo's bid for the presidency and the position of Federico Franco,
a medical doctor and a president of the PLRA, as the vice-presidential
candidate were formalized on 31 January 2008 at the offices of the TSJE
(Higher Tribunal for Electoral Justice) amid a show of popular support
from a big crowd. Lugo and Franco embraced, the former informally
dressed and without a tie, the latter in a grey suit with a grey tie.

The record of the TSJE was not such as to reassure candidates from
outside the ranks of the Colorados, and months of worry continued for
a candidate whose victory would put an end to sixty-one years of their
uninterrupted rule. They were divided but they could count on some
help from the store of knowledge of electoral trickery that they had
built up over the decades.

At the beginning of 2008 Duarte's candidate for the presidency
was confirmed. Blanca Margarita Ovelar, born in the northern city
of Concepción in 1957, a teacher by training and married with three
children, was minister of education and culture between 2002 and 2007.
Her simple message was that she was against poverty and would do
what she could to relieve it.

Meanwhile Oviedo still had his uses for the Colorados and the presidency, which was now in the hands of Duarte. As the date for the 2008

presidential elections approached, Duarte freed him from prison once again in March of that year, hoping that his freedom and the popularity he continued to enjoy would allow him to split the anti-government forces and thus torpedo Lugo's presidential hopes.

In *ABC Color*, Mabel Rehnfeldt, one of the paper's prominent reporters, told her readers of some other Colorado ruses. She pointed out that the only reason Methuselah – the man who, according to the Book of Genesis, lived to 969 – would not vote in Sunday's elections was that he had not taken out Paraguayan nationality. For years the Colorados had fixed it so that all state employees, including servicemen, automatically became Colorados whether they liked it or not. Dues to the party were automatically deducted from pay packets. Yet in its hour of need the Paraguayan establishment had to find new methods of cooking the books, not least with the elderly.

For instance, authorities at the polling station at Guayaybý, where he was duly registered, were awaiting Froilán Galeano Noguera, 140. At La Recoleta they had an eye out for Juan Weber, 122. At San Ignacio they were waiting for 111-year-old Elisa Quevedo. Among the 2.4 million registered voters confirmed by the country's Higher Court of Electoral Justice as having the vote, there were 100 centenarians and 7,700 aged ninety or above eligible to vote. Many old people were accompanied to the vote by shadowy figures who showed them how to express their preferences. Special attention was also given to the dead at polling time. The electoral authorities asserted trenchantly that many were hale and hearty and well able to carry out their civic duty.

For instance, Claudio Alejandro Martínez was twenty when six boys killed him early in 2007 for his shoes and his wallet. He was on the register. Eustacia Romero, a devoted Colorado party member, had died four years earlier at her home in Lambaré, a suburb of Asunción. But they had a voting slip ready for her at Caraguatay.

What is more, miracles could be wrought with one single registration. Mariano Alfonso, Susana Urbieta, María Manuela Bogarín and Cirila Medina Fernández all shared the same number on the electoral roll, viz. 57,524. Luckily there was no excuse for outrage or embarrassment; each of the four had the chance to vote at widely different polling stations and had no need to meet. There were nine instances of a single electoral number being shared by three electors, while there were 628 cases of one number serving two people.

Moreover, the people in charge of the voting register appeared to be promoting the cause of decongestion in Paraguay's crowded capital, Asunción. They transferred that city's voters – electorally at least –

to charming country villages. Take Yasy Cañy, a doubtless delightful settlement in the distant and remote department of Canindeyú. It did not exist in 2003. But suddenly it was called into life by the electoral authorities when 7,462 voters were put on its electoral register; 461 more went on to the list in 2006 and 1,042 the following year. Whether the 7,462 were actually living was not the point. The majority of the voters' names were just transferred from the capital.

Despite forebodings, polling day dawned promisingly and the sun went down to sounds of delight and rejoicing from the Lugo camp. As the results began to show increasing support for him, Blanca Ovelar did not take long to publicly acknowledge the obvious, and Oviedo did the same. Even Duarte had little alternative but to congratulate the people for the conduct of the election, while he insinuated that he was due a large part of the credit for the outbreak of democracy. 'For the first time in our history, one party will transfer power to another without a coup, without bloodshed and without fighting among brothers,' the president proclaimed.

ELECTORAL VICTORY

The final computation of the 1,874,127 votes cast gave Lugo 766,502 to Ovelar's 574,995, said the Electoral Commission. Despite – perhaps because of – his actions, Oviedo and his UNACE received 411,034, a figure that reflected the continuing admiration of many Paraguayans for a strong man in a uniform. Pedro Fadul, a talented leader of the left who had collected more than a fifth of the votes at the 2003 presidential election, picked up no more than 44,060, a miserable 2.4 per cent for his Partido Patria Querida (PPQ).

The joy of Lugo's supporters was tempered by the fact that, had the impossible happened and Ovelar and Oviedo come to terms on who was to stand on a unified Colorado platform, their combined vote of perhaps 1,000,000 might very well have carried the day against the total of less than 800,000 from the Lugo camp.

It was also clear that Lugo could not have won the day without the support of the Liberals and the presence of the PLRA's Federico Franco as his vice-presidential candidate. In the departments the PLRA candidates won seven of the seventeen governorships to the nine taken by the Colorados.

In the Upper House of Congress the Colorados lost one seat but nevertheless were the largest party, with fifteen of the forty-five seats, with the PLRA having fourteen, Oviedo's UNACE nine and Fadul's PPQ three.

That did not muffle the rejoicing in the Lugo camp. 'You are responsible for the happiness of the Paraguayan people today,' he said to cheering supporters as the results were announced. 'Today we can say that little people can also win. This is the Paraguay of my dreams. The Paraguay that is of all colours and all faces, everyone's Paraguay. This Lugo has a heart and he loves you a lot.'

Victory at the polls had immediate results at the Holy See.

On 30 June 2008, on the website of Lugo Presidente, appeared two news items, one accompanied by the photograph of a very happy president-elect, the other of Lugo laughing uproariously in the company of an equally merry Antonini on the sofa beside him in the Alianza's office. The first item recounted how the two men had met that day and the nuncio had read to Lugo the full text of the decree of 30 June 2008, which announced that Benedict XVI had agreed that Lugo should lose his clerical status and be released from his vows to the Society of the Divine Word, his obligation to celibacy and his other obligations under the Code of Canon Law.

Re's decree stated:

The recent situation that has come about with the election of Monsignor Fernando Lugo as President of the Republic of Paraguay demands a reconsideration, for the good of the country and in order to clearly and definitively distinguish between the office of President of the Republic and the exercise of the episcopal ministry, [of] the request he be allowed to set aside episcopal ministry and the clerical state.

Therefore having carefully examined all the circumstances His Holiness Benedict XVI ...

The use of white flags is unknown in Vatican diplomacy. Yet the rest of the message was tantamount to one. For his part Lugo accepted that the duties of president of the republic were incompatible with the ministry of a bishop and the clerical state.

In reality, the prohibition on a minister of the Church venturing into the world of high politics was not quite as unequivocal as it was presented by some spokesmen in the Vatican. To take one example, from time immemorial the joint sovereigns *ex officio* of the small Pyrenean principality of Andorra, now a prosperous tax haven, have been a Frenchman, currently the president of France, and a Spanish bishop. Monsignor Josef Tiso ruled Slovakia under German protection in the Second World War. Those situations never seemed to upset Vatican guardians of canon law.

In comments to the press after the poll the nuncio said that after five years Lugo could ask to be reappointed as a bishop and that he would in any case continue to be a priest because, according to the canon law of the Church, once you are a priest you stay a priest.

For his part the happy Lugo was quoted on his website as saying of the decree, 'Yes, it's been awaited for a long time. I'd like to thank His Holiness for a decision which hasn't been easy for the Vatican, because there are no precedents.' In making the new decision, Lugo said, Benedict had been thinking above all of the welfare of Paraguay.

A tricky operation had, it seemed, been pulled off with the minimum of damage to all concerned.

MORE HEADACHES FROM THE PARANÁ

Meanwhile the Itaipú affair continued to claim attention. In November 2000 President González Macchi and President Fernando Henrique Cardoso of Brazil had agreed that two more turbines would be installed to bring the scheme's capacity up to 14,000 MW. It would supply 95 per cent of the power consumed by 6 million Paraguayans and a quarter of that consumed by the nearly 200 million Brazilians.

The cost of Itaipú had now risen to about twice what it needed to cost, US$19 billion as against a more realistic price of US$9 billion. The exact figure quoted by EBI for 7 January 1999 was US$19,044,611,600, one half that sum attributable to construction costs and the other half going on the cost of borrowing the capital. Those members of the Paraguayan establishment who could establish a connection with those managing the scheme – not a difficult task in a society as small as theirs – joined up with their counterparts in Brazil and thought up ways of diverting some of the cash into their own pockets. One of the most important of these was President Juan Carlos Wasmosy.

He was followed in the presidency by Raúl Cubas Grau, a cement magnate and another well-known contractor for Itaipú who, in chaotic political circumstances, lasted only briefly in the presidency.

Confirming the wild overspending, Ricardo Canese, a former professor at the Catholic University who had to spend years in exile in Belgium for his opposition to the regime and who was appointed by President Lugo to be his strategist on the Itaipú question, commented in 1999, 'At the very most it should have cost no more than half what it has ended up costing.' The whole financial axis of the country was changed. 'Itaipú', said Canese, 'is the biggest project there has ever been in Paraguay. This society today revolves round the money that was made, honestly and dishonestly, out of Itaipú.' (The inflation of initial costs for large schemes was widely acknowledged in other countries of the world. The Channel Tunnel, for instance, was due to cost £2.6 billion at 1985 prices. The eventual price was 80 per cent more in real terms.)

The important question of the price paid by Brazil for the energy it received from Paraguay was put on the table in Brasília in the first working encounter Lugo had with Lula on 17 September 2008, a month after the Paraguayan's inauguration.

In previous months Lugo had expressed confidence about the outcome of talks. 'President Lula of Brazil has shown himself open to discussions about our concerns over Itaipú,' he said in an interview. 'Talks are scheduled and that fact means that everyone agrees there's a difficulty. We can sit around a table and agree on something better both for Brazil and for Paraguay.' At the same time he realized there were technical problems, such as the absence of transmission lines, which made it difficult for Paraguay to start using more of the power it had a right to.

Yet when talks did start in earnest, the Paraguayan side argued for an increase in price, which would bring into the country some US$2 billion. Brazil argued that there could be no renegotiation of the Itaipú treaty. That, Lula constantly repeated, would never get the approval of the Brazilian congress which such a move required.

The question of the Brasiguayos, people of Brazilian and Paraguayan origins living in eastern Paraguay, became one thorny new problem arising from Itaipú. The scheme brought a flood of new immigration from Brazil in the 1970s. The immigrants were productive and skilled farmers, and by the first years of the new century Paraguay had become the fourth-largest exporter of soya in the world, with 2.6 million hectares under the crop producing nearly 7 million tons of the bean every year.

The importance of the economic activity undertaken by the Brasiguayos was further underlined by the fact that in 2008 more than 40 per cent of the 8,500 cattle slaughtered every day for export in Paraguay passed through slaughterhouses – including the biggest one, which processed 1,600 head every day – which were owned by Brasiguayos.

Yet the Brasiguayos were at the same time at the bottom of a difficult political challenge for Lugo. In May 2008, on his return from the first international event he participated in after his electoral victory, the European Union–Latin America meeting of leaders in Lima, he went back to San Pedro to reinforce his commitment to agrarian reform and to those who were pushing for it. While in Lima he had heard of a confrontation between the landless and their champions on one side and the Brasiguayo ranchers and soya growers on the other. On 15 May demonstrators had burned a Brazilian flag at a farm at Curupayty. There was also a land invasion of a farm being worked by a Brasiguayo at Tapiracuái by members of the Mesa Coordinadora Nacional de Organizaciones Campesinas (MCNOC), the National Coordinating Board of Peasant Organizations, the main peasants' organization, formed in 1994 and a member of the APC which had a few days before brought him to power.

Elvio Benítez of the Coordinadora Productores Agrícolas San Pedro Norte, the Paraguayan farmers' association in the northern part of the department of San Pedro, who had organized the burning of the flag, went on to accuse the Brasiguayo settlers of 'poisoning the population' and illegally felling the forests. For Lugo this was a warning of the difficult situation he would doubtless face as he sought land reform, while at the same time seeking good relations with Paraguay's powerful neighbour to the east.

Meanwhile the situation at Yacyretá presented another difficult problem for Lugo as he took office. Argentina, so short of energy that power cuts had become routine there, was keen that the pending works at the Yacyretá dam be completed without delay, increasing the height of the dam from 78.5 to 83 metres and thus its capacity from 14 to 20 per cent of its requirements. That would help to alleviate the bottlenecks that were sapping the popularity of President Cristina Kirchner.

An investigation in 2004 showed that houses along the creeks around the city flooded every time it rained because of inadequate storm sewers and lack of town planning, and wells were polluted, resulting in an upsurge of diarrhoea, parasites, anaemia and skin rashes. The flooded-out homeowners had received none of the compensation promised by the Entidad Binacional Yacyretá (EBY), the body charged by the two countries with the construction and running of the scheme.

Complaints about non-payment arose on both sides of the river. In 2008 politics brought Lugo back in contact with the Argentine side, where Joaquin Piña, the retired Jesuit bishop of Puerto Iguazú, was playing an important part in mobilizing people to demand the compensation they had been pledged for their flooded lands.

Raising the water level to 83 metres demanded the flooding of an additional 55,000 hectares, to be added to the 110,000 hectares already under water behind the dam, most of which was on the Paraguayan side of the border. The EBY hoped to complete work on the Yacyretá project in 2009. But the question of compensation to be paid to the owners of flooded land was a brake on progress. At the beginning of 1999 *ABC Color* reported that one potential seller was asking the equivalent of £7,400 per hectare for land that normally went for £30 a hectare.

The asking price, 31 per cent higher than the highest official valuation, was supposedly demanded to allow the compensation of inhabitants who were somehow omitted from the census. In the days before his inauguration Lugo took the side of the Encarnacenos and said that the decision of the Colorado government in July 2008 to agree to the raising of the dam by 70 centimetres to 78.5 metres was irresponsible, and indeed called for an immediate reduction in the water level until the complementary works were completed, which would relieve what he called 'an environmental and health emergency'.

In similar circumstance to those at Itaipú, Paraguay consumed just 5 per cent of the energy generated by Yacyretá and sold the balance to Argentina at a price much lower than the market level. As he had with reference to Brazil, Lugo said he would renegotiate the price that Argentina paid for energy from the dam and expressed confidence in the outcome of the negotiations.

6 | A NEW PARAGUAY?

However skilful Lugo turned out to be, however well crafted the co-
alitions he was able to put together to run the country, no new president
– not even one as popular as the former bishop – could hope to be able
to haul Paraguay out of the quagmires in which history landed it. There
was, however, promise on the horizon.

The divisions among the races in Paraguay were deep, though the fact
that the use of Guaraní was well established at every level of society was
a hopeful sign. The development in the first years of the new century
of a lively debate among middle-class people about the degree to which
the use of Guaraní should be developed or even imposed promised
to be a fruitful one, despite the passionate arguments. Hopeful, too,
was the fact that there is in Paraguay little of the intense hatred of the
indigenes which is common in neighbouring Bolivia, particularly in the
prosperous eastern regions of the country, where some political leaders
have been eager to base their electioneering on outright hostility and
contempt for the Aymaras, the Quechuas and other peoples.

Paraguay was free, too, of memories of the hostilities between European settlers and the native people that coloured the history of Chile for
so many centuries, and which stain the pages of nineteenth-century history in Argentina. Slavery of the indigenes and forced labour were never
as widespread in Paraguay as they were in Brazil, Peru and Ecuador.

What is more, a new generation of politicians from Chávez to Morales
and Correa were changing the region's political discourse and throwing
racial questions open to consideration. The silence that President Cardoso of Brazil maintained on racial questions throughout his period of
office from 1995 to 2003 is seen by many as being difficult to understand
at the end of the first decade of the twenty-first century.

For all these reasons Lugo's concern for racial justice, which he
inherited from Las Casas and Gutiérrez and which was an integral part
of his liberation theology, did not appear as exotic during his term of
office as it might have appeared even late in the twentieth century.

In June 2007 Lugo set out his views about the Church in an interview
with *Página 12*, the Buenos Aires daily:

I believe that the Church is political, not for nothing was Jesus of Nazareth found guilty by two political courts and one religious one. But there's a fear that the Church is politicised, that the Church is mixed up with one particular historical project. The Church wants to preserve its history. In its pronouncements it's always been critical of totalitarianism, critical about the birth of capitalism and of socialism in its encyclicals from Leo XIII onward and that's still the case.

That did not totally quieten hostility from some of his erstwhile companions among the bishops. The ugly side of politics and religion was not long in showing itself when Bishop Livieres resumed his attacks on Lugo, whom he had previously written off as 'a dagger in the heart of the Church'.

In December 2008, from Ciudad del Este, *ABC*[20] reported him as saying that 'since the start of this government they have used various strategies to complicate my life'. This he put down to his firm opposition to liberation theology. He went on, 'For me the nub of the problem is liberation theology ... They say that the fact that I don't preach liberation theology means I'm against the people ... that I'm a priest with a conservative mentality. Well, I am doing what the Holy See tells me.'

The situation in Ciudad del Este was complicated by the presence of two priests of extreme conservative views who had been linked to the schismatic Lefebvrist movement in Argentina and the USA.

'THE BUBBLE OF SOLIDARITY'

The moderate social democracy of Lugo's 'twenty-first-century socialism' was beginning to become more accepted in a way it would not have been accepted during the lifetime of John Paul II and Ronald Reagan. Fixed financial orthodoxies such as had been put forward by supporters of the Washington Consensus were thoroughly shaken after the financial crisis of 2008/09 and the effective nationalization of private-sector banks even in the USA. The days of what Denis Healey, the British finance minister in the 1970s, termed 'sado-capitalism' were passing in a welter of banking and other corporate chaos.

There were tentative signs that the Vatican, too, shared these doubts about fixed financial orthodoxies. The very fact that Rome, having issued stern statements to the Paraguayan leader, decided finally that the two could come to terms was important in this context. Benedict indicated an armistice with Lugo by dispatching a pen to him as a gift.

---

20. *ABC Color*, 14 December 2008.

Lugo's victory was even seen by some as one of the harbingers of new social thinking from the Vatican. Sandro Magister, the well-informed columnist of *L'Espresso*, was speculating in December 2008 about the arrival of a new encyclical from Benedict XVI. Such a document was seen by some as essential if the Church's attitude to the shocks being delivered to capitalism by the tremors generated by the Wall Street crises and the collapse of so many banks in the USA was to be agreed, promulgated and perhaps accepted.

Magister said that *Centesimus Annus*, the encyclical proclaimed in 1991 by John Paul II, had never been seriously accepted by the Church as a whole because of its excessive friendliness towards the capitalist system as practised in the USA and its repeated warnings about the supposed sanctity of private property. Its author's concentration on the cold war and his apparent lukewarm appreciation of the problems of poorer countries came as no surprise given his conservatism on economic matters and his unwillingness to criticize a bastion of the West while a cold war was raging.

The crisis affecting US banks, which spread to other countries, combined with alarming signs of collapse in the US motor industry, did nothing to bolster the economic views of the late John Paul and favoured those, such as Lugo, who wanted reform.

In such circumstances, one of the main aims of the pontifical council for justice and peace headed by Cardinal Renato Martini was that of getting Benedict to issue a document more pertinent to the difficulties of poorer countries such as Paraguay. In such circumstances, too, the arrival of Ettore Gotti Tedeschi, an economist and president of the Italian subsidiary of Banco Santander Central Hispano, as a columnist for the Vatican newspaper *Osservatore Romano* – a man who was not averse to putting forward novel ideas about the future workings of the world economic system – was a potential harbinger of more up-to-date thoughts from the Vatican about the ways of the world.

On 5 December 2008 the front page of the *Osservatore Romano* carried a long piece by the banker which quietly mocked the efforts of the US government and others to reflate a faltering economy by orthodox methods. Rather than doing that, he wrote,

> ... why not consider a long-term bubble of solidarity, which would generate growth in production and manual labour by financing consumption and investment in poor countries? Which would permit, in a few years, about three billion people to participate in the growth of the entire economic system? These same people are

ready, immediately, to represent essential demand for the West, and to participate in projects for infrastructure and production, in projects for professional formation and scientific research.

This greater openness in the Vatican to new social thinking than John Paul II would have admitted was emphasized when *Osservatore Romano* put on the front page of its edition of 19 February 2009 an article by Gordon Brown, the British prime minister, which called for more international attention to the difficulties of poor countries and was in line with what Gotti Tedeschi had proposed. Brown declared that the moral case for action could not be stronger. He added:

> What this crisis has shown us is that we cannot allow problems to fester in one country: they will have a knock-on impact on all of us. It is therefore our collective responsibility to ensure that the needs of the poorest countries will not be an afterthought, tagged on due to moral obligation or guilt.

In a comment in the *Osservatore Romano* three days later the Italian banker said that Gordon Brown, 'the prime minister of a great nation', had delivered 'a magisterial lesson to anyone who wants to listen'. The importance of the failure of financial orthodoxy and uncertainty about what should come next were highlighted on the front page of the *Financial Times* of 7 March 2009. It announced a new series by well-known figures, including Lula, Paul Kennedy and Henry Paulson, in the following week's newspaper: 'On Monday the FT begins a major series on the future of capitalism. The credit crunch has destroyed faith in the free market ideology that has dominated western economic thinking for a generation. But what should replace it?'

In Paraguay the question remained: would the bishop-turned-president have sufficient skill to take advantage of the political currents that seemed destined to carry him along? Would Lugo's victory be a turning point in his country's painful history?

As he settled into office Fernando Lugo could look back on the undeniable results of several years of hectic activity. He had put an end to sixty-one years of uninterrupted rule by the Colorados. As a man whose financial honesty was unquestioned, he had set a new example in a country where corruption was the rule and thereby had begun the task of making Paraguay a country to be taken seriously. He had started to honour his promise to educate the richer Paraguayans in the realization that mass poverty was not their ally but a threat to their future. In a region that had had more than its fill of tyrants, many of whose leaders were pushing ahead with reform of society, Lugo was joining in a continent-wide campaign.

In his interview with *Página 12* in January 2009 he marvelled at the pace of change in Latin America – and in the Middle East following the Israeli attack on Gaza in the days after Christmas 2008 – since 2001 and the time of the first World Social Forum.

> Who was going to imagine, not eight years ago but one year ago, that the struggle of social movements, of young people, of indigenes, of women, of workers was to yield such fruit? The struggle of the social movements is the great support of an enduring change in the region. A few years back our countries had conservative governments which we defeated. But that is not enough. A change in ethics is needed. And we must go back to believing in the prophecy of the Guaraní people, that of the 'Land without Evil'. We've had successes and blunders. So we've to proclaim some things with great clarity. For instance what we feel when we see murdered Palestininan children.

He was starting to exorcize the evil ghost of Alfredo Stroessner and with his friends was beginning to cure the rot in the society of Latin America. That in itself was a victory.

POSTSCRIPT: MOTHERS AND CHILDREN

Few political ambushes can ever have been better prepared; in few can the victim have been caught in a more vulnerable position. It all happened during Holy Week, the days before Easter 2009, one of the most solemn ceremonies in the Church's liturgical year, which also coincided with the first anniversary of Lugo's victory at the polls. Traps laid by the president's opponents – notably among the Colorados but also among the Liberals within his Alliance for Change – to have Lugo revealed as the father of a number of children born illegitimately to a succession of mothers over a number of years, were sprung.

The first public report of Lugo having been the father of a child came during Easter weekend 2009, when Viviana Carrillo, twenty-six, announced she was seeking his acknowledgement that he had sired Guillermo Armindo, who was shortly to celebrate his second birthday. On Monday, 13 April, the president called a press conference in Asunción and admitted he was the father of the boy, announcing that the official register, as a judge had ordered, would be amended, adding Lugo's name as father to recognize that fact. Carrillo, for her part, added that Lugo was 'pleased with his son' and 'constantly kept up with his activities'.

In a press conference rapidly called in the presidential palace, he declared, 'It is true that there was a relationship with Viviana Carrillo. In the light of that I assume all the responsibilities which could flow from such a fact, recognizing the paternity of the boy. From now on, respecting the boy's privacy and the high responsibilities which the exercise of the presidency imposes on me, I shall make no more statements on the subject.'

In an interview with the Madrid daily *ABC* he added that the fact would not weaken him politically. 'No, I don't believe so. One has to be faithful to those more than 800,000 people who voted for me. It is possible that the political class take advantage of a case of this nature and they can inflate its importance and blow it up.'

That same day Benigna Leguizamón, twenty-seven, a former cleaner from San Pedro now living with a partner in Ciudad del Este and the mother of four children, demanded DNA testing of the president and the acknowledgement of his paternity of her son Lucas Fernando, six.

On Wednesday, 22 April the Paraguayan *ABC* carried an item about a third woman, Damiana Hortensia Morán Amarilla, thirty-nine, who was a former coordinator of pastoral outreach in the San Pedro diocese. A woman with political experience in Tekejoja, she now worked in a nursery and canteen for children in a poor part of Asunción. The father of her son, Juan Pablo, sixteen months old and named by her after Pope John Paul II, was, she claimed, also Lugo. Press reports said she was divorced after seventeen years of marriage, which had produced two other children. Talking to reporters, she said she had learned a month or so previously that a list was being prepared of six women who claimed that the president had fathered children with them and who were to make a joint claim that he should assume his parental duties.

When asked whether she and Lugo were still in love, she replied, 'I can tell you about my feelings, but I want to respect his. But what I feel up to now is just that, love.'

A fourth woman, Raquel Torres from San Pedro, living in Spain and working in domestic service, was reported also to have had a girl, now four, with Lugo, whom she had left with family in Paraguay. She refused to answer questions about the child's paternity.

The Colorado president, Senator Lilian Samaniego, made much of the cases, fleetingly charging Lugo with '*estupro*' or rape, a charge, later retracted, which relates to having sex with an underage girl. (Though this charge was never made by the Colorados against their leader Stroessner, who, for many decades, made this his principal leisure activity.)

Various opposition figures piled on allegations that he was 'an abuser who abused the confidence of those who blindly voted for him', that he was 'not a good priest, is not a good president, is not a good father, nor is he a good friend'. A leading Colorado figure said, 'As a woman I say that Lugo has toyed with the dignity of various Paraguayan women and toyed with the dignity of the people' – again, never a charge levelled against Stroessner.

The identities of the remaining two women supposedly on Morán's list continued to be the subject of speculation as the opposition sought to keep the balloon of scandal inflated.

For their part, Lugo's allies, including Liz Torres, the secretary for children, and her cabinet colleague Gloria Rubín, secretary for women, promoted the view that his recognition of Guillermo Armindo as his son was 'an act of courage'.

A week after the first announcement the president declared in another press conference, 'I have no problem in asking pardon when I recognize that I have failed the Church, the country, the citizens, those who gave me their confidence,' adding, 'I make my confession to my confessors.' He was firm in declaring that he would on no account resign from the presidency, adding that he would make every effort to bring about 'a dramatic protection of effort on all questions concerning motherhood, children and women' in the government's agenda.

The declaration further strained the already tense relations between Lugo and his vice-president, Federico Franco, who announced at the time of the revelations that he was 'perfectly prepared' to assume the presidency, which, according to the constitution, he would inherit if Lugo resigned. He added cautiously that he would not seek a role in any impeachment of the president.

From Brasília, Lugo received the political support of Lula, the Brazilian president, who announced that he could see no reason for there to be a constitutional crisis in Paraguay. At the summit meeting of American presidents and heads of government in Port of Spain later that month he met Barack Obama and other notables from the continent.

A very large proportion of Paraguayans are born outside marriage. In a poor diocese such as San Pedro, where, as we have seen, eighteen priests had charge of 350,000 Catholics, the task of organizing the blessing of all marriages would in itself be immense. In such a poor country many have difficulty in finding the time and the cash, however minimal, to celebrate nuptials. The Buenos Aires daily *Clarín* claimed on 26 April that in the ten years to 2002 more than 200,000 births had not been registered in Paraguay and, out of every ten registrations of new births, seven were submitted by unmarried mothers. Consequently, the reactions among Paraguayans to the news was a complex one. Few expressed approval of the appearance of yet more fatherless offspring in their country, this time sired by a bishop apparently with a strong taste for promiscuity. Among those with enough money to stage well-financed weddings there were expressions of horror, stoked by the opposition for all they were worth. Poorer people – those who formed the bulk of Lugo's supporters on polling day – who expected to benefit by the reforms he stood for and whose relationships never made it to the society pages of the newspapers, made less fuss.

An added factor, which, for a long time, had influenced sexual relations and attitudes to marriage in Paraguay, was the continuing effect of the War of the Triple Alliance in the 1860s and the resultant holocaust, which had shorn the country of all but 28,000 of its men. History textbooks tell of Paraguay's pre-war population of 1,300,000 being reduced to 200,000 by the end of the war, of which only 10 per cent were male, most of whom were children, old men or foreigners. The effort to contribute to a regrowth of the population was seen as a national duty for years thereafter.

For its part, the Paraguayan Church and its bishops were thrown into confusion by the events surrounding Lugo. Lugo's friend and ally, Bishop Mario Medina of San Ignacio, underlined his 'bravery', while Bishop Rogelio Livieres, a member of Opus Dei, was caustically critical. Livieres's diocese, Ciudad del Este, had given assistance to various extreme right-wing members of the Saint Pius X Society who were known for their hostility to women's rights and even to their continuing education. Livieres asserted that the bishops had known all about Lugo's sexual activities and had kept silent about them. This brought a strong response from the Paraguayan Bishops' Commission, which said it 'lamented and rejected' Livieres's remarks and asserted that they had learned of Lugo's resignation from his diocese only when it was announced that the pope had accepted it in January 2005. The Vatican maintained a discreet silence on the matter.

Yet the affair had ramifications in the wider world beyond Paraguay. One of the most striking commentaries from Latin America came in *Valores Religiosos*, a supplement, edited by the archbishopric of Buenos Aires, to the Buenos Aires daily *Clarín*. In an article at the beginning of May 2009, two priests considered the impact of Lugo's action on the debate in the Church about the obligation of celibacy, which has for centuries been imposed on priests of the Latin rite, but not on those of the various oriental rites in communion with Rome. Celibacy was also optional for priests in the Orthodox churches owing allegiance not to Rome but to the Orthodox patriarch – based in Constantinople, now Istanbul – the successor to the leaders of the ancient Greek church of Byzantium.

The authors of the *Valores Religiosos* article pointed out that the question of obligatory celibacy had long been preoccupying priests and that many in Argentina had dared to say it should be optional, not least given the fact that even the apostle Peter was a married man. Yet Benedict XVI had banned all such discussion. The authors quoted Bishop Joaquín Piña – the septuagenarian Jesuit bishop emeritus of the Argentine diocese of Puerto Iguazú on the Paraná river, and a battler along with Lugo for improved rights for the poor of that region – as saying 'one has to accept that we are human and we can fall down on celibacy which is not a divine mandate but something imposed by the church'.

Farinello, one of the authors, himself confessed, 'I fell in love when I was 30 and I know that it's not easy to maintain the faithfulness that the church imposes.' He added, 'Benedict XVI is a conservative, a man of some years who has a nostalgic view of what the faith was in Europe.'

Both authors pointed out that in recent times 150,000 priests had left the priesthood to get married.

Jesus didn't mention celibacy and in fact among his apostles were single men and married men, said Farinello. 'Peter on whom the church was built had a wife. Celibacy is a gift, a charism, and no one can be against such a formidable undertaking. But I believe that it should be an option for those priests who want a family.'

The article in *Valores Religiosos* owed much to a recent one published in another Argentine publication, *Veintitrés*, on 30 April 2009, which carried the views of five Argentine priests who strongly questioned the refusal of the Vatican to reconsider the duty of celibacy imposed on priests of the Latin rite.

The *Veintitrés* article recalled how Cardinal Carlo Martini, the former archbishop of Milan who obtained the highest vote in the consistory of cardinals meeting in Rome to elect a pope to succeed John Paul II in 2005, but who had turned down the papacy on health grounds, had expressed a preference for voluntary celibacy.

Lugo's case was reminiscent of that of Bishop Jerónimo Podestá of the Argentine diocese of Avellaneda, although the circumstances were very distinct. The Podestá case lacked the overtones of promiscuity that apparently surrounded the Lugo case, yet one could not fail to echo the other.

The five priests also recalled how it had been Podestá who had been the first in recent times to announce that he was in love. In 1966 he had met Clelia Luro, the mother of six daughters. She became his secretary and the two lived unashamedly together until he was suspended by Rome from his diocese a year later. He went to Rome accompanied by Clelia to plead his case personally, but in vain. The couple returned to Argentina, where she wore his episcopal ring on her finger.

After receiving death threats from the far right the two went into exile in 1974, and Podestá became president of the Latin American Federation of Married Priests and Their Wives.

As the affair of the former bishop and his progeny rumbled on it seemed that Fernando Armindo Lugo's actions were adding fuel to the flames of the worldwide debate on celibacy, which Benedict had tried to suppress. His conduct and his politics meant that history would be unlikely to forget the doings of the priest from Paraguay.

BIBLIOGRAPHY

Paraguay

Alegre Ortiz, Heriberto (1987) *La Sociedad Cautiva*, Asunción: Comisión de Defensa de los Derechos Humanos del Paraguay.

Andrada Nogués, Luis Manuel (2008) *La Rebeldía de Lugo y la Mitra Abandonada; Monseñor Fernando Lugo Méndez, Obispo Emérito de San Pedro*, Asunción: Editorial Tiempo Nuevo.

Azara, Félix de (1847) *Descripción e historia del Paraguay y del Río de la Plata*, Madrid: Sánchiz.

Bethell, Leslie (1996) *The Paraguayan War (1864–1870)*, London: University of London Institute of Latin American Studies Research Papers 46.

Bourgade la Dardye, Emmanuel de (n.d.), *Paraguay: The land and the people, natural wealth and commercial capabilities*, London: G. Philip.

Caraman, Philip, SJ (1975), *The Lost Paradise: An account of the Jesuits in Paraguay, 1607–1768*, London: Sidgwick and Jackson.

Cardozo, Efraim (2007) *Apuntes de Historia Cultural del Paraguay*, 8th edn, Asunción: Servilibro.

Carver, Robert (2007) *Paradise with Serpents*, London: HarperCollins.

Cunninghame Graham, R. B. (1924) *A Vanished Arcadia*, London: Heinemann.

Duviols, Jean-Paul and Rubén Barreiro Saguier (eds) (1991) *Tentación de la Utopía; las Misiones Jesuíticas del Paraguay*, Barcelona.

Enríquez Gamón, Efraín (1994) *Francia, un Hombre Interminable*, Asunción: El Lector.

Estigarribia, José Félix (1972) *La Epopea del Chaco*, Asunción: Ministerio de Hacienda.

Frings, Paul and Josef Übelmesser (1982) *Paracuaria, Art Treasures of the Jesuit Republic of Paraguay*, Mainz: Matthias-Grünewald-Verlag.

Frutos, Julio César and Helio Vera (1998) *Elecciones 1998; Tradición y Modernidad*, Asunción: Editorial Medusa.

Greene, Graham (1969) *Travels with My Aunt*, London: Bodley Head.

— (1973) *The Honorary Consul*, London: Bodley Head.

Lambert, Peter and Andrew Nickson (eds) (1997) *The Transition to Democracy in Paraguay*, Basingstoke: Palgrave Macmillan.

Livingstone, Grace (2009) *America's Backyard: The United States and Latin America from the Monroe Doctrine to the War on Terror*, London: Zed Books.

McNaspy, Clement J., SJ (1987) *Una Visita a las Ruinas Jesuíticas*, Asunción: Centro de Estudios Paraguayos 'Antonio Guasch'.

Melià Lliteras, Bartolomeu, SJ (1988) *Una Nación, Dos Culturas*, Asunción: RP Ediciones CEPAG.

Miranda, Aníbal (1957) *EEUU y*

el Regimen Militar Paraguayo (1954–1958), Asunción: El Lector.

Montaigne, Michel de (2004) *The Complete Essays*, London: Penguin.

Mora, Frank and Jerry Cooney (2007) *Paraguay and the United States: Distant Allies*, Athens: University of Georgia.

Neri Farina, Bernardo (2003) *El Último Supremo*, Asunción: El Lector.

Painter, James (1983) *Paraguay in the 1970s: Continuity and Change in the Political Process*, London: University of London Institute of Latin American Studies Working Papers 9.

Pitaud, Henri (1978) *Madama Lynch* (translated from French), Asunción: Editorial France-Paraguay.

Pastor Benítez, Justo (1942) *Estigarribia, el Soldado del Chaco*, Asunción: Carlos Schauman Editor.

Rivarola, Milda, José Carlos Rodríguez, Juan Andrés Cardozo and Andrés Colman Gutiérrez (2001) *Marzo Paraguayo, una lección de democracia*, Asunción: Biblioteca Ultima Hora.

Roa Bastos, Augusto (1974) *Yo, el supremo*, Barcelona: Plaza y Janés Editores.

— (1977) *Cándido López*, Milan: Franco Maria Ricci.

Robertson, J. P. and W. P. (1838) *Letters on Paraguay*, London.

Vaconsellos, Victor Natalicio (1970) *Lecciones de Historia Paraguaya*, 6th edn, Asunción: published by author.

Vera, Saro (1996) *El Paraguayo (un hombre fuera de su mundo)*, Asunción: El Lector.

Zook, David H., Jr (1960) *The Conduct of the Chaco War*, New Haven, CT: Bookman Associates.

Catholic Church

Annuario Pontificio (annually) *Libreria Editrice Vaticana*, Vatican City, with much of its material accessible on the US website www.catholic-hierarchy.org.

Cavallo, Ascanio (ed.) (1999) *Memorias: Cardenal Raúl Silva Enríquez*, Santiago: Ediciones Copygraph.

Filochowski, Julian (1992) *Archbishop Romero*, London: Catholic Institute for International Relations.

Goldman, Francisco (2008) *The Art of Political Murder: Who Killed Bishop Gerardi?*, London: Atlantic.

Gutiérrez, Gustavo (1988) *A Theology of Liberation*, London: SCM.

Hebblethwaite, Peter (1984) *John XXIII, Pope of the Council*, London: Geoffrey Chapman.

Linden, Ian (2009) *Global Catholicism: Diversity and Change since Vatican II*, London: Hurst & Co.

Luis Jerónimo (1607) *Rituale, su Manuale Peruanum et forma brevis adminstrandi apud Indios sacrosancta Baptismi, Poenitenciae, Eucharistiae, Matrimonii et Extremae Unctionis Sacramenta*, Naples.

Novak, Michael (1964) *The Open Church; Vatican II Act II*, London: Darton, Longman and Todd.

REMHI (1999) *Guatemala Never Again! The Official Report of the Human Rights Office of the Archdiocese of Guatemala*, Maryknoll, NY, and London: Maryknoll/Catholic Institute for International Relations/Latin America Bureau.

Roncagliolo, Rafael and Fernando Reyes Matta (1978) *Iglesia, Prensa y Militares – el Caso Riobamba y los Obispos Latinoamericanos*, Mexico City: Instituto Latinoamericano de Estudios Transnacionales.

Rowland, Christopher (ed.) (1999) *The Cambridge Companion to*

Liberation Theology, Cambridge: Cambridge University Press.

Sobrino, Jon (2008) *The Eye of the Needle*, London: Darton, Longman and Todd.

Verbitsky, Horacio (2005) *El Silencio; de Paulo VI a Bergoglio: Las Relaciones Secretas de la Iglesia con la ESMA*, Buenos Aires: Sudamericana.

— (2006) *Doble Juego: la Argentina Católica y Militar*, Buenos Aires: Sudamericana.

Whitfield, Teresa (1994) *Paying the Price: Ignacio Ellacuría and the Murdered Jesuits of El Salvador*, Philadelphia, PA: Temple University Press.

Miscellaneous

Baum, Dan (1996) *Smoke and Mirrors: The War on Drugs and the Politics of Failure*, Boston, MA: Little, Brown & Co.

Bethell, Leslie (ed.) (1984–2009) *Cambridge History of Latin America*, 12 vols, Cambridge: Cambridge University Press.

Bonner, Raymond (1984) *Weakness and Deceit: US Policy and El Salvador*, New York: Times Books.

Dunkerley, James (1988) *Power in the Isthmus: A Political History of Modern Central America*, London: Verso.

Iriarte, Gregorio, OMI (2007) *Análisis Crítico de la Realidad*, 16th edn, La Paz: Grupo Editorial Kipus.

O'Shaughnessy, Hugh (2000) *Pinochet, the Politics of Torture*, London/ New York: Latin America Bureau/ New York University Press.

Preston, Ronald H. (1979) *Religion and the Persistence of Capitalism*, London: SCM Press.

Newspapers

ABC Color, Asunción; *La Nación*, Asunción; *Última Hora*, Asunción; *Clarín*, Buenos Aires; *Página 12*, Buenos Aires; *O Estado de S. Paulo*; *Globo*, Rio de Janeiro

INDEX